W9-BKM-059

The Italian and Northern Renaissance

POWER AND RELIGION IN MEDIEVAL AND RENAISSANCE TIMES

THE ITALIAN AND NORTHERN RENAISSANCE

EDITED BY KELLY ROSCOE

Published in 2018 by Britannica Educational Publishing (a trademark of Encyclopædia Britannica, Inc.) in association with The Rosen Publishing Group, Inc.
29 East 21st Street, New York, NY 10010

Distributed exclusively by Rosen Publishing.
To see additional Britannica Educational Publishing titles, go to rosenpublishing.com.

First Edition

Britannica Educational Publishing
J.E. Luebering: Executive Director, Core Editorial
Andrea R. Field: Managing Editor, Compton's by Britannica

Rosen Publishing
Meredith Day: Editor
Nelson Sá: Art Director
Brian Garvey: Designer
Cindy Reiman: Photography Manager
Bruce Donnola: Photo Researcher

Library of Congress Cataloging-in-Publication Data
Names: Roscoe, Kelly, editor.
Title: The Italian and northern Renaissance / edited by Kelly Roscoe.
Description: First edition. | New York : Britannica Educational Publishing in association with Rosen Educational Services, 2018. | Series: Power and religion in medieval and Renaissance times | Includes bibliographical references and index.
Identifiers: LCCN 2016053738 | ISBN 9781680486278 (library bound : alkaline paper)
Subjects: LCSH: Renaissance--Italy--Juvenile literature. | Renaissance--Europe, Northern--Juvenile literature. | Italy--Intellectual life--1268-1559--Juvenile literature. | Europe, Northern--Intellectual life--Juvenile literature.
Classification: LCC DG445 .I74 2018 | DDC 940.2/1--dc23
LC record available at https://lccn.loc.gov/2016053738

Manufactured in China

Photo credits: Cover, pp. 3, 12, 26, 42, 57, 77 Conde/Shutterstock.com; pp. 8-9, 82 © Photos.com/Thinkstock; pp. 14 DEA/G. Dagli Orti/De Agostini/Getty Images; p. 18 Scala/Art Resource, New York; pp. 20-21 Universal Images Group/Hulton Fine Art Collection/Getty Images; p. 23 Fototeca Storica Nazionale/Hulton Archive/Getty Images; pp. 24-25 Palazzo Vecchio (Palazzo della Signoria) Florence, Italy/Bridgeman Images; p. 27 DEA/Pinaider/De Agostini/Getty Images; p. 29 Print Collector/Hulton Archive/Getty Images; p. 31 Photo12/Universal Images Group/Getty Images; p. 35 DEA/A. Dagli Orti/De Agostini/Getty Images; pp. 38, 50-51, 55, 90 De Agostini Picture Library/Getty Images; p. 40 Mondadori Portfolio/Hulton Fine Art Collection/ Getty Images; p. 45 Imagno/Hulton Fine Art Collection/Getty Images; pp. 46-47 Laura Lezza/Getty Images; pp. 50-51, 55, 90 DEA Picture Library/De Agostini/Getty Images; p. 52 DEA/Veneranda Biblioteca Ambrosiana/De Agostini/Getty Images; p. 59 Leemage/Corbis Historical/Getty Images; pp. 60-61 © Collection of the Earl of Pembroke, Wilton House, Wilts./Bridgeman Images; pp. 62-63, 75 PHAS/Universal Images Group/Getty Images; p. 65 Heritage Images/Hulton Fine Art Collection/Getty Images; pp. 66-67 Universal History Archive/Universal Images Group/Getty Images; p. 70 Giraudon/Art Resource, New York; p. 73 Universal Images Group/Getty Images; pp. 78-79 Bibliotheque Nationale, Paris, France/Archives Charmet/Bridgeman Images; p. 84 Library of Congress, Washington, D.C. (file no. LC-USZ62-110330); p. 86 Private Collection/Photo © Christie's Images/ Bridgeman Images; p. 88 Leemage/Universal Images Group/Getty Images; interior pages background and border graphics Roberto Castillo/Shutterstock.com; back cover flourish Drakonova/Shutterstock.com

Contents

Introduction

The modern period of history is often considered to have begun with the Renaissance, one of the rare periods of genius in the world's history. It immediately followed the period in Europe known as the Middle Ages. The Renaissance began in Italy during the late 13th and early 14th centuries and reached its height in the 15th. In the 16th and 17th centuries it spread to the rest of Europe.

The word "renaissance" means "rebirth." It refers to the rediscovery by scholars (primarily grouped under the heading of humanists) of the cultural heritage of the ancient Greeks and Romans. In fact, however, the Renaissance was a period of discovery in many fields—of new scientific laws, new forms of art and literature, new religious and political ideas, and new lands, including America.

The term "Middle Ages" was coined by scholars in the 15th century

In his fresco *The School of Philosophy*, the Renaissance painter Raphael depicts an imaginary meeting of Plato and Aristotle (framed by the small arch, *centre*) with other philosophers from all periods of history.

to designate the interval between the downfall of the Classical world of Greece and Rome and its rediscovery at the beginning of their own century, a revival in which they felt they were participating. Indeed, the notion of a long period of cultural darkness had been expressed by Petrarch even earlier. Events at the end of the Middle Ages, particularly beginning in the 12th century, set in motion a series of social, political, and intellectual transformations that culminated in the Renaissance. These included the increasing failure of the Roman Catholic Church and the Holy Roman Empire to provide a stable and unifying framework for the organization of spiritual and material life, the rise in importance of city-states and national monarchies, the development of national languages, and the breakup of the old feudal structures.

While the spirit of the Renaissance ultimately took many forms, it was expressed earliest by the intellectual movement called humanism. Humanism was initiated by secular men of letters rather than by the scholar-clerics who had dominated medieval intellectual life and had developed the Scholastic philosophy. Humanism began and achieved fruition first in Italy. Its predecessors were men like Dante and Petrarch, and its chief protagonists included Gianozzo Manetti, Leonardo Bruni, Marsilio Ficino, Giovanni Pico della Mirandola, Lorenzo Valla, and Coluccio Salutati. The fall of Constantinople in 1453 provided humanism with a major boost, for many eastern scholars fled to Italy, bringing with them important books and manuscripts and a tradition of Greek scholarship.

Now few historians are comfortable with the triumphalist and western Euro-centred image of the Renaissance as the irresistible march of modernity and progress. The older view of the Renaissance centred too exclusively on Italy, and within Italy on a few cities—Florence, Venice, and Rome. Nevertheless, the term "Renaissance" remains a widely recognized label for the multifaceted period between the heyday of medieval universalism, as embodied in the papacy and Holy Roman Empire, and the convulsions and sweeping transformations of the 17th century.

In this period, some important innovations of the Middle Ages came into their own, including the revival of urban life, commercial enterprise based on private capital, banking, the formation of states, systematic investigation of the physical world, Classical scholarship, and vernacular literatures. In religious life, the Renaissance was a time of the broadening and institutionalizing of earlier initiatives in lay piety and lay-sponsored clerical reforms, rather than of the abandonment of traditional beliefs. In government, city-states and regional and national principalities supplanted the fading hegemony of the empire and the papacy and obliterated many of the local feudal jurisdictions that had covered Europe. Within states, though, power continued to be monopolized by elites who drew their strength from both landed and mercantile wealth.

Chapter One

Urban Growth and Wars of Expansion

Town revival was a general feature of 10th- and 11th-century Europe (associated with an upsurge in population that is not completely understood). In Italy, however, the urban imprint of Roman times had never been erased. By the 11th century, the towers of new towns, and, more commonly, of old towns newly revived, began to dot the spiny Italian landscape. The burgeoning population was literally brimming with new energy due to improved diets. As in Roman times, the medieval Italian town lived in close relation to its surrounding rural area, or *contado*.

Italian city folk seldom relinquished their ties to the land from which they and their families had sprung. Most successful tradesmen or bankers would invest some of their profits in the family farm, while rural nobles often spent part of the year in houses inside city walls. In Italian towns, knights, merchants, rentiers, and skilled craftsmen lived and worked side by side, fought in the same militia, and married into each other's families. Though there was a social hierarchy, it was a tangled system with no simple division between noble and commoner, between landed and commercial wealth.

Civic Institutions

The fact that landed nobles took part in civic affairs helps explain the early militancy of the townsfolk in resisting the local bishop, who was usually the principal claimant to lordship in the community. Political action against a common enemy tended to infuse townspeople with a sense of community and civic loyalty. By the end of the 11th century, civic patriotism began to express itself in literature. City chronicles combined fact and legend to stress a city's Roman origins and, in some cases, its inheritance of Rome's special mission to rule. Such motifs reflect the cities' achievement of autonomy from their respective episcopal or secular feudal overlords and, probably, the growth of rivalries between neighbouring communities.

Rivalry between towns was part of the expansion into the neighbouring countryside, with the smaller and weaker towns submitting to the domination of the larger and stronger. As the activity of the towns became more complex, permanent civic institutions began to emerge. Typically, the first of these was an executive magistracy, named the consulate (to stress the continuity with republican Rome). In the late 11th and early 12th centuries, this process consisted of the establishment of juridical autonomy, the emergence of a permanent officialdom, and the spread of power beyond the walls of the city to the *contado* and neighbouring towns.

Siena, the seal of which is seen here, became an important banking centre in the 13th century but was unable to compete with its rival, Florence.

About a dozen Italian centres had developed these institutions, while others were beginning the process. The loose urban community was becoming a corporate entity, or commune; the city was becoming a city-state.

The typical 13th-century city-state was a republic administering a territory of dependent towns; whether it was a democracy is a question of definition. The idea of popular sovereignty existed in political thought and was reflected in the practice of calling a *parlamento,* or mass meeting, of the populace in times of emergency. However, none of the republics allowed the people as a whole to have regular participation in government. On the other hand, the 13th century saw the establishment, after considerable struggle, of assemblies in which some portion of the male citizenry, restricted by property and other qualifications, took part in debate, legislation, and the selection of officials. Most offices were filled by men serving on a rotating, short-term basis. Also, most men were obligated to serve in the civic militia. But the degree of participation in public life varied from one commune to another and tended to decline. Most of the city republics were small enough so that public business was conducted by and for citizens who knew each other, and civic issues were a matter of widespread and intense personal concern. In 1300 Florence, with perhaps 100,000 people, was one of the largest republics; most were about the size of Padua, which had about 15,000 people.

Civic Strife and One-Man Rule

The darker side of this intense community life was conflict. It became a cliché of contemporary observers that when townsmen were not fighting their neighbours they were fighting each other. Machiavelli explained this as the result of the natural enmity between nobles and "the people—the former desiring to command, the latter unwilling to obey."

GUELFS AND GHIBELLINES

Guelfs (also spelled Guelphs), who were sympathetic to the papacy, and Ghibellines, who were sympathetic to the German (Holy Roman) emperors, were members of two opposing factions in German and Italian politics. The split between the two groups contributed to chronic strife within the cities of northern Italy in the 13th and 14th centuries.

Guelf was derived from Welf, the name of the dynasty of German dukes of Bavaria who competed for the imperial throne through the 12th and early 13th centuries. The name *Ghibelline* was derived from Waiblingen, the name of a castle of the Welfs' opponents, the Hohenstaufen dukes of Swabia. The Ghibellines' most famous member was the Hohenstaufen emperor Frederick I Barbarossa (1152–90), who tried to reassert imperial authority over northern Italy by force of arms. Frederick's military expeditions were opposed not only by the Lombard and Tuscan communes, who wished to preserve their autonomy within the empire, but also by the newly elected (1159) pope Alexander III. Frederick's attempts to gain control over Italy thus split the peninsula between those who sought to enhance their powers and prerogatives by siding with the emperor and those (including the popes) who opposed any imperial interference.

The struggles between the Hohenstaufen emperor Frederick II (reigned 1220–50) and the popes often contributed to intensifying antagonisms within and among the Italian cities. The rivalry between Ghibellines (in this case representing feudal aristocrats) and Guelfs (representing wealthy merchants) was especially ferocious in Florence, where the Guelfs were exiled twice (1248 and 1260) before the invading Charles of Anjou ended Ghibelline domination in 1266. A series of wars was fought from the mid-13th century through the early 14th century between Guelf-controlled Florence and its allies—Montepulciano, Bologna, and Orvieto—and its Ghibelline opponents—Pisa, Siena, Pistoia, and Arezzo.

After the Hohenstaufen loss of southern Italy (1266) and the final extinction of their line (1268), the Guelf and Ghibelline conflict changed in meaning. In the international sphere, Guelfism constituted a system of alliances among those who supported the Angevin presence in southern Italy—including the Angevin rulers of Sicily themselves, the popes, and Florence with its Tuscan allies. Within the many cities where the Guelfs triumphed, the party became a conservative force, a property-owning group interested in maintaining the exile of the Ghibellines whose holdings had been confiscated. Ghibellinism became associated with nostalgia for the empire (a waning force in Italy after 1268) and briefly revived during the Italian expeditions of the emperors Henry VII in 1310–13 and Louis IV in 1327–30.

During the course of the 14th century, the importance of both parties rapidly declined. They lost international significance because the emperors no longer interfered in Italy and the popes moved from Rome to France. "Guelf" and "Ghibelline" implied only local factions.

The unequal distribution of power and privilege was a problem, but this class division was further complicated by factional rivalry within the ruling groups and by ideological differences—Guelfism, or loyalty to the pope, versus Ghibellinism, or loyalty to the German emperors. The continuing leadership of the old knightly class, with its violent feudal ways and the persistence of a winner-take-all conception of politics, guaranteed bloody and devastating conflict. Losers could expect to be condemned to exile, with their houses burned and their property confiscated. Winners had to be forever vigilant against the unending conspiracies of exiles yearning to return to their homes and families.

During the 14th century, a number of cities, despairing of finding a solution to the problem of civic strife, were turning from republicanism to *signoria*, the rule of one man. The *signore*, or lord, was usually a member of a local feudal family that was also a power in the commune. Thus, lordship did not appear to be an abnormal development, particularly if the signore chose, as most did, to rule through existing republican institutions. Sometimes a *signoria* was established as the result of one noble faction's victory over another. In a few cases a feudal noble who had been hired by the republic as its *condottiere*, or military captain, became its master. Whatever the process, by the late 14th century hereditary lordship was much more common than free republicanism. The signori were so successful in controlling the areas of administration, justice, and the military that historians have considered them to be among the originators of the modern state.

Miracle of the True Cross at the Bridge of S. Lorenzo, oil painting of Venice by Gentile Bellini, 1500

Italy in the 14th century had not shaken off feudalism.

In the south, feudalism was entrenched in the loosely centralized Kingdom of Naples, successor state to the Hohenstaufen and Norman kingdoms. In central and northern Italy, feudal lordship and knightly values merged with medieval communal institutions to produce the typical state of the Renaissance. Parliamentary republicanism had a longer life in places where the nobles were excluded by law from political participation in the commune, such as the Tuscan cities of Florence, Siena, Pisa, and Lucca. But even these bastions of liberty had intervals of disguised or open lordship. The great maritime republic of Venice reversed the usual process by increasing the powers of its councils at the expense of the doge (from Latin *dux*, "leader"). However, Venice never had a feudal nobility, only a merchant aristocracy that called itself noble and jealously guarded its hereditary sovereignty against incursions from below.

New Functions of the City-State

There were new as well as traditional elements in the Renaissance city-state. Changes in the political and economic situation affected the evolution of government, while the growth of the humanist movement influenced developing conceptions of citizenship, patriotism, and civic history. Both the empire and the papacy were not able to dominate Italian affairs as they had done in the past, which left each state free to pursue its own goals within the limits of its resources. These goals were, invariably, the security and power of each state in regard to its neighbours. Diplomacy became a skilled game of experts; rivalries were deadly, and warfare was endemic.

This 14th-century fresco depicts merchants in Siena. Trade and banking both helped transform Italian city-states around this time.

Because the costs of war were all-consuming, particularly as mercenary troops replaced citizen militias, the states had to find new sources of revenue and develop methods of securing public credit. Governments borrowed from moneylenders (stimulating the development of banking), imposed customs duties, and levied fines. But, as their costs continued to exceed revenues, they came up with new solutions such as the forced loan, funded debt, and taxes on property and income. New officials with special skills were required to take property censuses (the *catasto*), calculate assessments, and manage budgets. They also had to provision troops, take minutes of council meetings, administer justice, write to other governments, and send instructions to envoys and other agents. All this required public space—council, judicial, and secretarial rooms, storage space for bulging archives, and both closed and open-air ceremonial settings where officials interacted with the citizenry and received foreign visitors.

As secular needs joined and blended with religious ones, towns took their place alongside the church and the monasteries as patrons of builders, painters, and sculptors (often the same persons). In the late 13th century, great programs of public building and decoration were begun. These were intended to symbolize and portray images of civic power and beneficence and to communicate the values of "the common good." Thus, the expansion of the functions of the city-state was accompanied by the development of a public ideology and a civic rhetoric intended to make people conscious of their blessings and responsibilities as citizens.

The city-state tended to absorb many of the protective and associative functions and loyalties connected with clan, family, guild, and party. Some historians have claimed that the city-state fostered individualism by replacing traditional forms of association, but this assessment is problematic. The Renaissance "discovery of the individual" is a vague concept, lending itself to many different meanings. It could be argued, for example, that the development of communal law, with its strong Roman influence, enhanced individual property rights or that participatory government promoted a consciousness of individual value. It could also be argued, however, that the city-state was a more effective controller of the loyalty and property of its members than were feudal jurisdictions and voluntary associations. In some respects the great merchants and bankers of the Renaissance, operating in international markets, had more freedom than local tradespeople, who were subject to guild restrictions, communal price and quality controls, and usury laws. However, the economic ideal of Renaissance states was mercantilism, not free private enterprise.

Wars of Expansion

Amid the confusion of medieval Italian politics, a new pattern of relations emerged by the 14th century. No longer revolving in the papal or in the imperial orbit, the stronger states were free to assert their dominance over the weaker, and a system of regional power centres evolved. From time to time the more ambitious states, especially those that

The Visconti family, whose coat of arms is shown here, dominated the history of northern Italy in the 14th and 15th centuries.

had brought domestic conflict under control, made a bid for a wider control in the peninsula. For example, Milan attempted to expand under the lordship of the Visconti

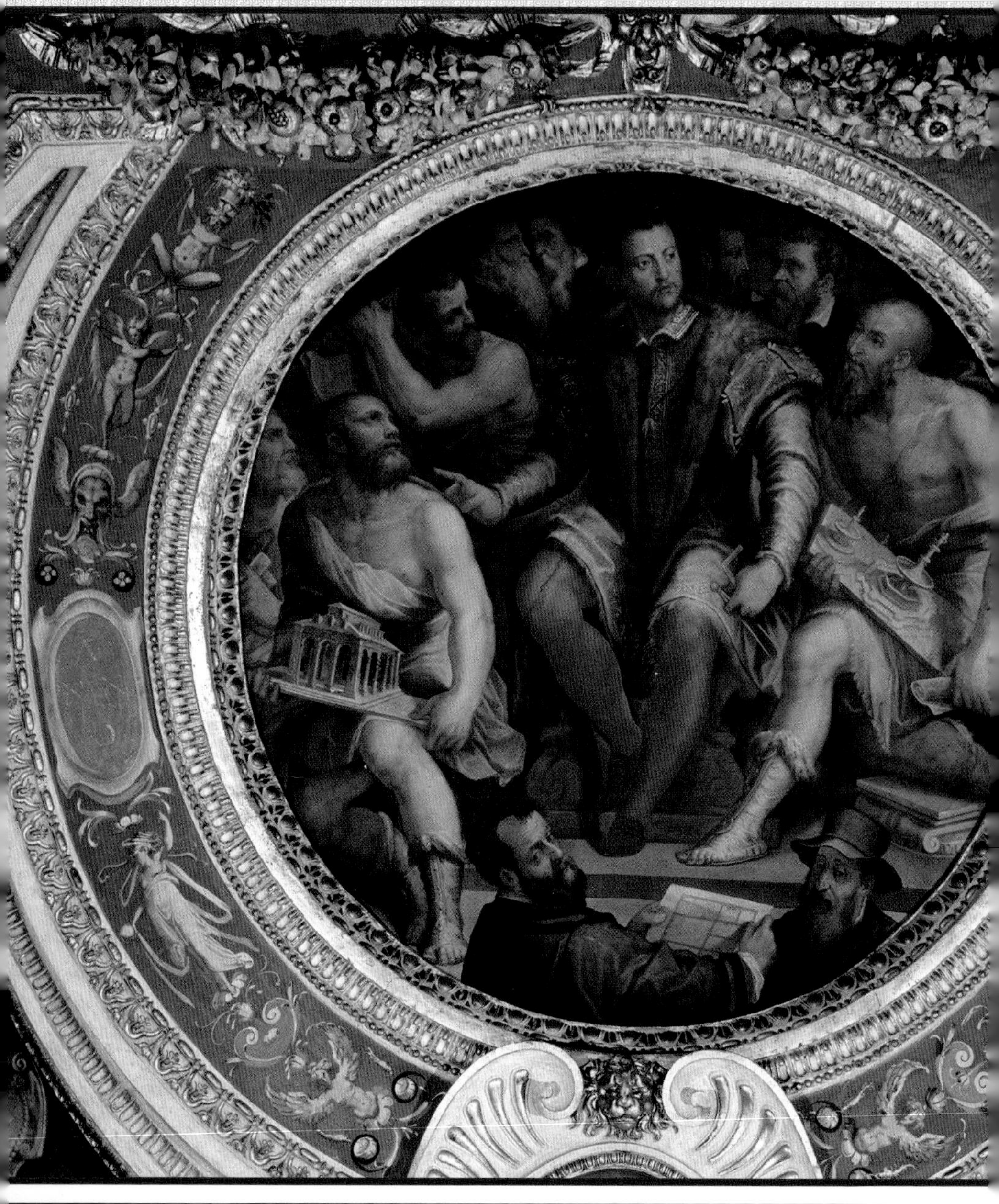

This 16th-century painting shows Cosimo de' Medici alongside artists he patronized.

family. In the 1380s and '90s Gian Galeazzo Visconti pushed Milanese power eastward as far as Padua, at the very doorstep of Venice, and southward to the Tuscan cities of Lucca, Pisa, and Siena and even to Perugia in papal territory. Some believed that Gian Galeazzo meant to be king of Italy. Whether or not this is true, he would probably have overrun Florence, the last outpost of resistance in central Italy, had he not died suddenly in 1402, leaving a divided inheritance and much confusion.

In the 1420s, under Filippo Maria, Milan began to expand again. By then, though, Venice, with territorial ambitions of its own, had joined with Florence to block Milan's advance, while the other Italian states took sides or remained neutral according to their own interests. The mid-15th century saw the Italian peninsula embroiled in a turmoil of intrigues, plots, revolts, wars, and shifting alliances. The most sensational alliance was the reversal that brought the two old enemies, Florence and Milan, together against Venetian expansion. This "diplomatic revolution," supported by Cosimo de' Medici, the unofficial head of the Florentine republic, is the most significant illustration of the emergence of balance-of-power diplomacy in Renaissance Italy.

Chapter Two

Italian Humanism

he idea that classical thought and wisdom was not revived until the Renaissance is a myth. Like all such myths, it is a blend of fact and invention. Classical thought and style permeated medieval culture in ways past counting. Most of the authors known to the Renaissance were known to the Middle Ages as well, while the Classical texts "discovered" by the humanists were often not originals but medieval copies preserved in monastic or cathedral libraries.

Moreover, the Middle Ages had produced at least two earlier revivals of Classical antiquity. The so-called Carolingian Renaissance of the late 8th and 9th centuries saved many ancient works from destruction or oblivion, passing them down to posterity in its beautiful minuscule script (which influenced the humanist scripts of the Renaissance). A 12th-century Renaissance saw the revival of Roman law, Latin poetry, and Greek science, including almost all of

ἈΡΙΣΤΟΤΈΛΟΥΣ ἨΘΙΚΩ͂Ν
ΝΙΚΟΜΑΧΕΙΩΝ Θ

This page of Aristotle's *Nichomachean Ethics*, written *c.* 350 BCE, comes from a 10th-century manuscript.

Aristotle's known writings. Nevertheless, the Classical revival of the Italian Renaissance was so different from these earlier movements in spirit and substance that the humanists might justifiably claim that it was original and unique.

LITERACY AND LANGUAGE

During most of the Middle Ages, Classical studies and virtually all intellectual activities were carried on by churchmen, usually members of the monastic orders. Italian cities boasted literate lay people who had a taste and need for literary culture. New professions reflected the growth of both literary and specialized lay education—the *dictatores,* or teachers of practical rhetoric, lawyers, and the ever-present notary (a combination of solicitor and public recorder). These were the true predecessors of the humanists.

In Padua a kind of early humanism emerged, flourished, and declined between the late 13th and early 14th centuries. Paduan classicism was a product of the vigorous republican life of the commune, and its decline coincided with the loss of the city's liberty. A group of Paduan jurists, lawyers, and notaries—all trained as *dictatores*—developed a taste for Classical literature that probably stemmed from their professional interest in Roman law and their affinity for the history of the Roman Republic. The most famous of these Paduan classicists was Albertino Mussato, a poet, historian, and playwright, as well as lawyer and politician. His play *Ecerinis,* modeled on Seneca, has been called the first Renaissance tragedy.

By reviving several types of ancient literary forms and by promoting the use of Classical models for poetry and rhetoric, the Paduan humanists helped make the 14th-century

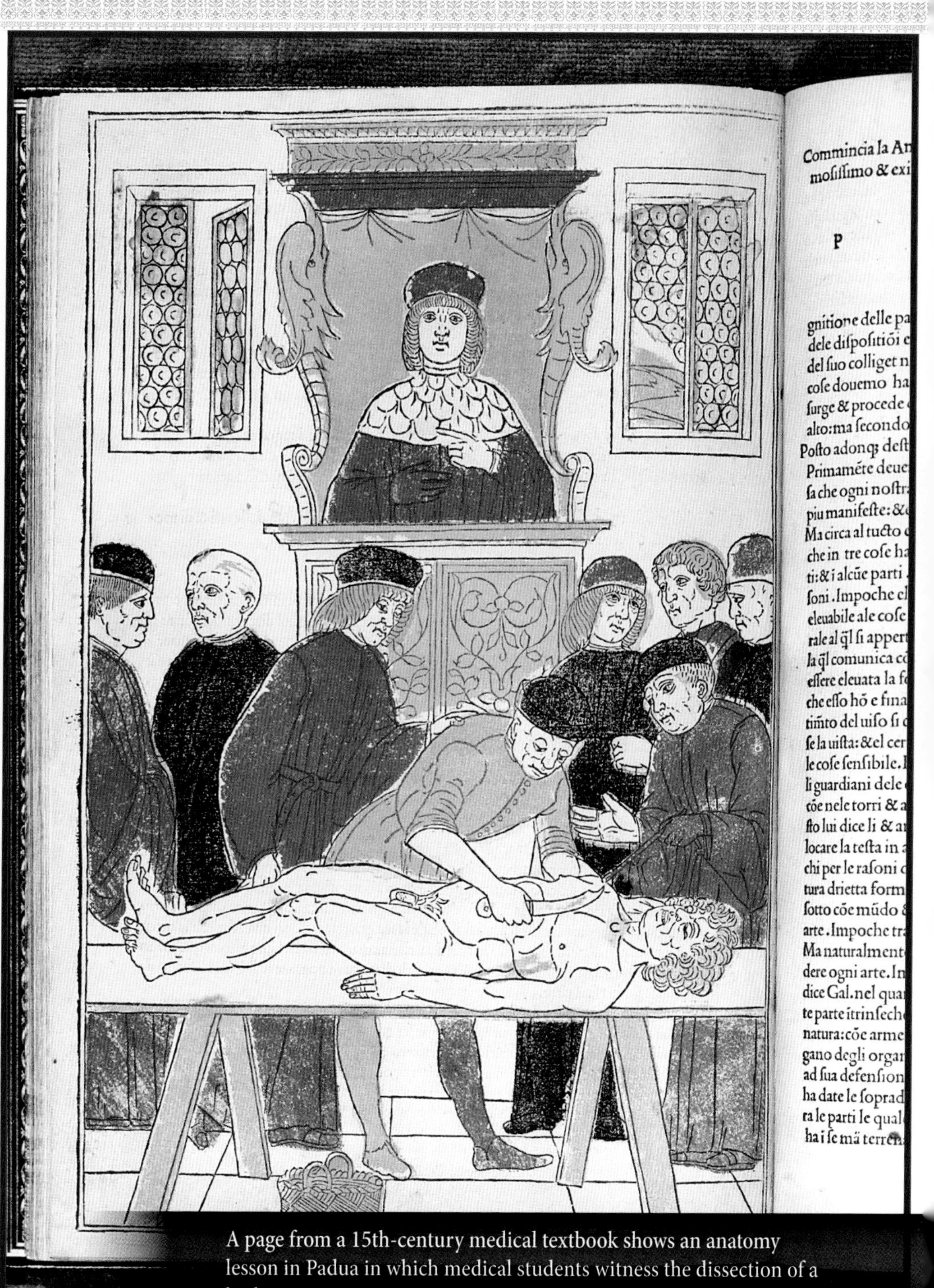

A page from a 15th-century medical textbook shows an anatomy lesson in Padua in which medical students witness the dissection of a body.

Italians more conscious of their Classical heritage. In other respects, however, they remained close to their medieval predecessors, showing little comprehension of the vast cultural and historical gulf that separated them from the ancients.

It was Francesco Petrarca, or Petrarch, who first understood fully that antiquity was a civilization apart and, understanding it, outlined a program of Classically oriented studies that would lay bare its spirit. The focus of Petrarch's insight was language: if Classical antiquity was to be understood in its own terms, it would be through the speech with which the ancients had communicated their thoughts. This meant that the languages of antiquity had to be studied as the ancients had used them and not as vehicles for carrying modern thoughts. Thus, grammar, which included the reading and careful imitation of ancient authors from a linguistic point of view, was the basis of Petrarch's entire program.

From the mastery of language, one moved on to the attainment of eloquence. For Petrarch, as for Cicero, eloquence was not merely the possession of an elegant style, nor yet the power of persuasion, but the union of elegance and power together with virtue. One who studied language and rhetoric in the tradition of the great orators of antiquity did so for a moral purpose—to persuade men and women to the good life. As Petrarch said in a statement that could stand as the slogan of Renaissance humanism, "it is better to will the good than to know the truth."

The Humanities

To will the good, one must first know it, and so there could be no true eloquence without wisdom. According to

Petrarch's poems addressed to Laura, an idealized beloved, contributed to the flowering of lyric poetry during the Renaissance.

Petrarch

The Italian poet and scholar Francesco Petrarca, more commonly known as Petrarch, was one of the key figures of the Renaissance. Through his fascination with, and intense study of, the writings of ancient Greece and Rome, he became convinced there was a continuity between classical culture and Christianity. By trying to weave the two together into a common tradition, Petrarch became the founder of humanism.

Petrarch was born in Arezzo, Tuscany, on July 20, 1304. In 1312 his family moved to Avignon, France, the temporary site of the papal court. There, he made valuable contacts in the church, and he used the city of nearby Vaucluse as his base until 1353, when he settled in Italy. Petrarch's father sent him to study law in Montpellier, France, in 1316, and he was not able to abandon the subject until his father died in 1326. He returned to Italy to continue his legal studies at Bologna in 1320 but was already becoming fascinated with literature. Petrarch's earliest surviving poems, on the death of his mother, date from this period. Once free of law he pursued the study of classical literature and his relentless search for ancient manuscripts. One of his significant discoveries, at Verona in 1345, was a collection of the letters of the Roman orator Cicero.

Petrarch produced a sizable number of writings. The most celebrated are the poems collectively called "Rime" (Rhymes), which tell of the great love of his life: a woman named Laura, whom he first saw in church on April 6, 1327. She has never been identified. Among his other works are "Africa," an epic poem about the Second Punic War; "De viris illustribus" (Illustrious Men), a series of biographies; "Secretum meum" (My Secret), an autobiographical series of imaginary dialogues with St. Augustine; "De vita solitaria" (The Life of Solitude); "Epistolae metricae" (Letters in Verse); and "Trionfi" (Triumphs), a poem on the progress of the soul from Earth to heaven.

In 1353 Petrarch went to live in Italy permanently. By 1367 he had settled in Padua. He died in nearby Arqua on July 19, 1374.

Leonardo Bruni, a leading humanist of the next generation, Petrarch "opened the way for us to show in what manner we might acquire learning." Petrarch's union of rhetoric and philosophy, modeled on the Classical ideal of eloquence, provided the humanists with an intellectual dignity and a moral ethos lacking to the medieval *dictatores* and classicists. It also pointed the way toward a program of studies—the *studia humanitatis*—by which the ideal might be achieved. As elaborated by Bruni, Pier Paolo Vergerio, and others, the notion of the humanities was based on Classical models—the tradition of a liberal arts curriculum conceived by the Greeks and elaborated by Cicero and Quintilian.

Medieval scholars had been fascinated by the notion that there were seven liberal arts, no more and no less, although they did not always agree as to which they were. The humanists had their own favorites, which invariably included grammar, rhetoric, poetry, moral philosophy, and history, with a nod or two toward music and mathematics. They also had their own ideas about methods of teaching and study. They insisted upon the mastery of Classical Latin and, where possible, Greek, which began to be studied again in the West in 1397, when the Greek scholar Manuel Chrysoloras was invited to lecture in Florence. They also insisted upon the study of Classical authors at first hand, banishing medieval textbooks from their schools. This greatly increased the demand for Classical texts, which was first met by copying manuscript books in the newly developed humanistic scripts and then, after the mid-15th century, by the method of printing with movable type, first developed in Germany and rapidly adopted in Italy and elsewhere. Thus, while it is true that most of the ancient authors were already known in the Middle Ages, their works were often jealously guarded as a prized possession in some remote monastery library. Now, however, these books were circulated in many copies to a reading public.

The term "humanist" (Italian *umanista*, Latin *humanista*) first occurs in 15th-century documents to refer to a teacher of the humanities. Humanists taught in a variety of ways. Some founded their own schools—as Vittorino da Feltre did in Mantua in 1423 and Guarino Veronese in Ferrara in 1429—where students could study the new curriculum at both elementary and advanced levels. Some humanists taught in universities, which, while remaining strongholds of specialization in law, medicine, and theology, had begun to make a place for the new disciplines by the late 14th century. Still, others were employed in private households. For example, the poet and scholar Politian (Angelo Poliziano), was tutor to the Medici children as well as a university professor.

Formal education was only one of several ways in which the humanists shaped the minds of their age. Many were themselves fine literary artists who exemplified the eloquence they were trying to foster in their students. Renaissance Latin poetry, for example, contains much graceful and lyrical expression by such humanists as Politian, Giovanni Pontano and Jacopo Sannazzaro. In drama,

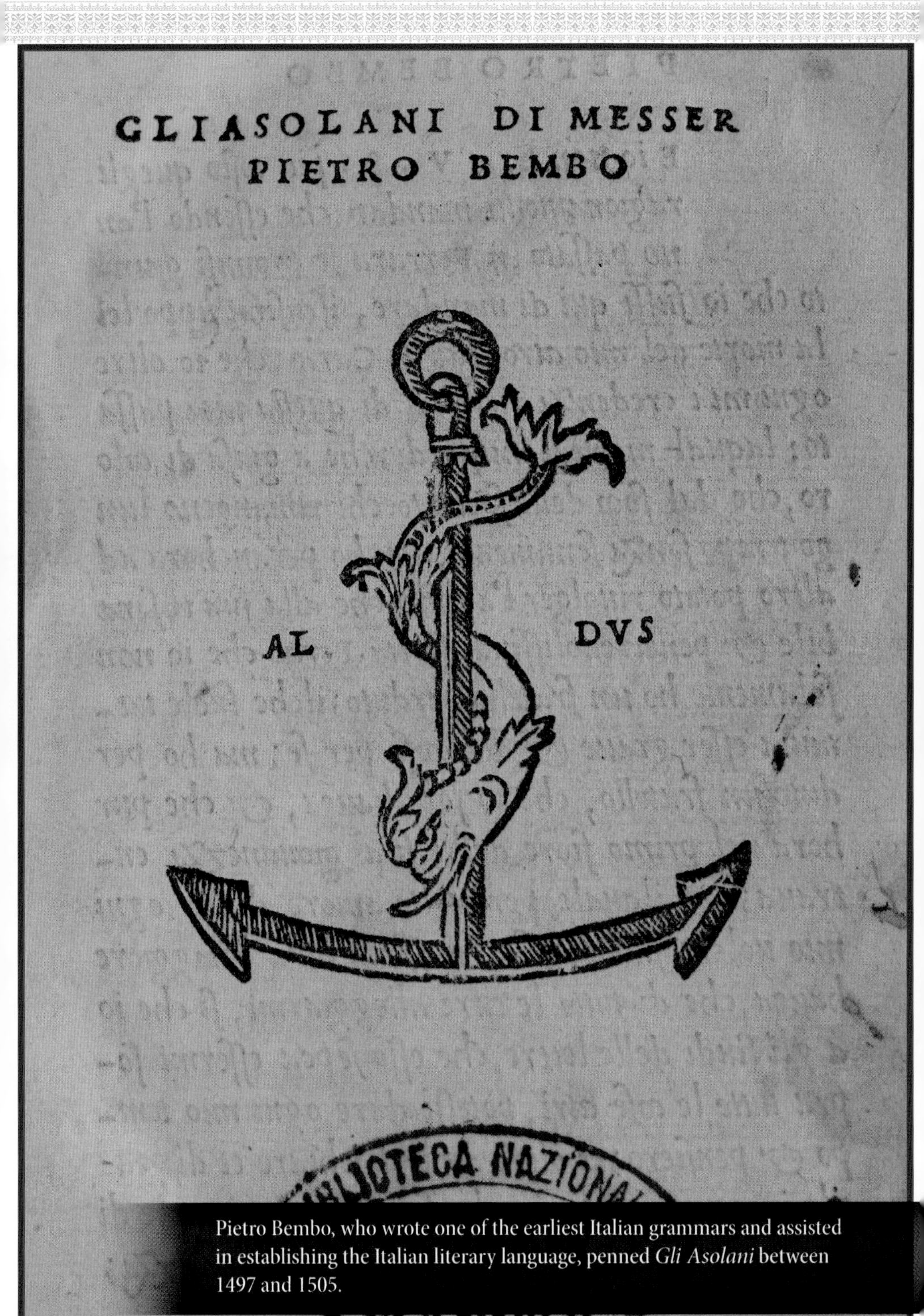

Pietro Bembo, who wrote one of the earliest Italian grammars and assisted in establishing the Italian literary language, penned *Gli Asolani* between 1497 and 1505.

Politian, Pontano and Pietro Bembo were important innovators, and the humanists were in their element in the composition of elegant letters, dialogues, and discourses. By the late 15th century, humanists were beginning to apply their ideas about language and literature to composition in Italian as well as in Latin, demonstrating that the "vulgar" tongue could be as supple and as elegant in poetry and prose as was Classical Latin.

Classical Scholarship

Not every humanist was a poet, but most were classical scholars. Classical scholarship consisted of a set of related, specialized techniques by which the cultural heritage of antiquity was made available for convenient use. Essentially, in addition to searching out and authenticating ancient authors and works, this meant editing—comparing variant manuscripts of a work, correcting faulty or doubtful passages, and commenting in notes or in separate treatises on the style, meaning, and context of an author's thought. Obviously, this demanded not only superb mastery of the languages involved and a command of Classical literature but also a knowledge of the culture that formed the ancient author's mind and influenced his writing. Consequently, the humanists created a vast scholarly literature devoted to these matters and instructive in the critical techniques of classical philology, the study of ancient texts.

Classicism and the literary impulse went hand in hand. From Lovato Lovati and Albertino Mussato to Politian and Pontano, humanists wrote Latin poetry and drama with considerable grace and power. Others composed epistles, essays, dialogues, treatises, and histories on Classical models. In fact, it is fair to say that the development of elegant prose was the major literary achievement of humanism and that the epistle was its typical form. Petrarch's practice of collecting, reordering, and even rewriting his letters—of treating them as works of art—was widely imitated.

For lengthier discussions, the humanist was likely to compose a formal treatise or a dialogue—a Classical form that provided the opportunity to combine literary imagination with the discussion of weighty matters. The most famous example of this type is *The Courtier,* published by Baldassare Castiglione in 1528. It was a graceful discussion of love, courtly manners, and the ideal education for a perfect gentleman, and it had enormous influence throughout Europe. Castiglione had a humanist education, but he wrote *The Courtier* in Italian, the language Bembo chose for his dialogue on love, *Gli Asolani* (1505), and Ludovico Ariosto chose for his delightful epic, *Orlando furioso,* completed in 1516. The vernacular was coming of age as a literary medium.

According to some, a life-and-death struggle between Latin and Italian began in the 14th century, while the mortal enemies of Italian were the humanists, who impeded the natural growth of the vernacular after its brilliant beginning with Dante, Petrarch, and Giovanni Boccaccio. In this view, the choice of Italian by such great 16th-century writers as Castiglione, Ariosto, and Machiavelli represents the final triumph of the vernacular and the restoration of contact between Renaissance culture and its native roots. The reality is somewhat less dramatic and more complicated. Most Italian writers regarded Latin as being as much a part of their culture as the vernacular, and most of them wrote in both languages. It should also be remembered that Italy was a land of powerful

This illustrated page from Dante's *The Divine Comedy* (written c. 1308–21) dates from a 14th-century printing.

regional dialect traditions; until the late 13th century, Latin was the only language common to all Italians. By the end of that century, however, Tuscan was emerging as the primary vernacular, and Dante's choice of it for his *The Divine Comedy* ensured its preeminence. Of lyric poets writing in Tuscan (hereafter called Italian), the greatest was Petrarch. His *canzoni*, or songs, and sonnets in praise of Laura are revealing studies of the effect of love upon the lover; his *Italia mia* is a plea for peace that evokes the beauties of his native land; his religious songs reveal his deep spiritual feeling.

Petrarch's friend and admirer Giovanni Boccaccio is best known for his *Decameron*. He also pioneered in adapting Classical forms to Italian usage, including the hunting poem, romance, idyll, and pastoral. Some of his themes, most notably the story of Troilus and Cressida, were borrowed by other poets, including Geoffrey Chaucer and Torquato Tasso.

The scarcity of first-rate Italian poetry throughout most of the 15th century has caused a number of historians to regret the passing of *il buon secolo*, the great age of the language, which supposedly came to an end with the ascendancy of humanist Classicism. For every humanist who disdained the vernacular, however, there was a Leonardo Bruni to maintain its excellence or a Poggio Bracciolini to prove it in his own Italian writings. Indeed, there was an absence of first-rate Latin poets until the late 15th century, which suggests a general lack of poetic creativity in this period and not of Italian poetry alone. It may be that both Italian and Latin poets needed time to absorb and assimilate the various new tendencies of the preceding period. Tuscan was as much a new language for many as was Classical Latin, and there was a variety of literary forms to be mastered.

Lorenzo de' Medici ruled Florence with his younger brother, Giuliano (1453–78), from 1469 to 1478 and, after the latter's assassination, was sole ruler from 1478 to 1492.

With Lorenzo de' Medici the period of tutelage came to an end. The Magnificent Lorenzo, virtual ruler of Florence in the late 15th century, was one of the finest poets of his time. His sonnets show Petrarch's influence, but transformed with his own genius. His poetry epitomizes the Renaissance ideal of *l'uomo universale*, the many-sided man. Love of nature, love of women, and love of life are the principal themes. The woodland settings and hunting scenes of Lorenzo's poems suggest how he found relief from a busy public life; his love songs to his mistresses and his bawdy carnival ballads show the other face of a devoted father and affectionate husband. The celebration of youth in his most famous poem was etched with the sad realization of the brevity of life; his own ended at the age of 43:

> *Oh, how fair is youth, and yet how fleeting! Let yourself be joyous if you feel it: Of tomorrow there is no certainty.*

Florence was only one centre of the flowering of the vernacular. Ferrara saw literature and art flourish under the patronage of the ruling Este family. Before the end of the 15th century Ferrara had at least one major poet, Matteo Boiardo, author of the *Orlando innamorato*, an epic of Roland. A blending of the Arthurian and Carolingian epic traditions, Boiardo's *Orlando* inspired Ludovico Ariosto to take up the same themes. The result was the finest of all Italian epics, *Orlando furioso*. The ability of the medieval epic and folk traditions to inspire the poets of such sophisticated centres as Florence and Ferrara suggests that, humanist disdain for the Dark Ages notwithstanding, Renaissance Italians did not allow Classicism to cut them off from their medieval roots.

Chapter Three

Renaissance Thought

While the humanists were not primarily philosophers and belonged to no single school of formal thought, they had a great deal of influence upon philosophy. They searched out and copied the works of ancient authors, developed critical tools for establishing accurate texts from variant manuscripts, made translations from Latin and Greek, and wrote commentaries that reflected their broad learning and their new standards and points of view. Aristotle's authority remained preeminent, especially in logic and physics, but humanists were instrumental in the revival of other Greek scientists and other ancient philosophies, including stoicism, skepticism, and various forms of Platonism, as, for example, the eclectic Neoplatonist and Gnostic doctrines of the Alexandrian schools known as Hermetic philosophy. All of these were to have far-reaching effects on the subsequent development of European thought. While humanists had a variety of intellectual and scholarly aims, it is fair to say that, like the ancient Romans, they preferred moral philosophy to metaphysics. Their faith in the moral benefits of poetry and rhetoric inspired generations of scholars and educators. Their emphasis upon eloquence, worldly achievement, and fame brought them readers and patrons among merchants and princes and employment in government chancelleries and embassies.

Humanists were secularists in the sense that language, literature, politics, and history, rather than "sacred subjects," were their central interests. They defended themselves against charges from conservatives that their preference for Classical authors was ruining Christian morals and faith, arguing that a solid grounding in the classics was the best preparation for the Christian life. This was already a perennial debate, almost as old as Christianity itself, with neither side able to prove its case. There seems to have been little atheism or dechristianization among the humanists or their pupils, although there were efforts to redefine the relationship between religious and secular culture. Petrarch struggled with the problem in his book *Secretum meum* (1342–43, revised 1353–58), in which he imagines himself chastised by St. Augustine for his pursuit of worldly fame. Even the most celebrated of Renaissance themes, the "dignity of man," best known in the *Oration* (1486) of Giovanni Pico della Mirandola, was derived in part from the Church Fathers. Created in the image and likeness of God, people were free to shape their destiny, but human destiny was defined within a Christian, Neoplatonic context of contemplative thought.

MACHIAVELLI AND *THE PRINCE*

Perhaps because Italian politics were so intense and innovative, the tension between traditional Christian teachings and actual behaviour was more frankly acknowledged in political thought than in most other fields. The leading spokesman of the new approach to politics was Niccolò Machiavelli. Best known as the author of *The Prince* (1513), a short treatise on how to acquire power, create a state, and keep it, Machiavelli dared to argue that success in politics had its own rules. This so shocked his readers that they coined his name into synonyms for the Devil ("Old Nick") and for crafty, unscrupulous tactics (Machiavellian). No other name, except perhaps that of the Borgias, so readily evokes the image of the wicked Renaissance, and, indeed, Cesare Borgia was one of Machiavelli's chief models for *The Prince*.

Machiavelli began with the not unchristian axiom that people are immoderate in their ambitions and desires and likely to oppress each other whenever free to do so. To get them to limit their selfishness and act for the common good should be the lofty, almost holy, purpose of governments. How to establish and maintain governments that do this was the central problem of politics, made acute for Machiavelli by the twin disasters of his time, the decline of free government in the city-states and the overrunning of Italy by French, German, and Spanish armies. In *The Prince* he advocated his emergency solution: Italy needed a new leader, who would unify the people, drive out "the barbarians," and reestablish civic virtue. But in the *Discourses on the First Ten Books of Livy* (1517), a more detached and extended discussion, he analyzed the foundations and practice of republican

Niccolò Machiavelli, a political philosopher and statesman, gained a reputation as an atheist and an immoral cynic from his most famous work, *The Prince*.

government, still trying to explain how stubborn and defective human material was transformed into political community.

Machiavelli was influenced by humanist culture in many ways, including his reverence for Classical antiquity, his concern with politics, and his effort to evaluate the impact of fortune as against free choice in human life. The "new path" in politics that he announced in *The Prince* was an effort to provide a guide for political action based on the lessons of history and his own experience as a foreign secretary in Florence. In his passionate republicanism he showed himself to be the heir of the great humanists of a century earlier who had expounded the ideals of free citizenship and explored the uses of Classicism for the public life.

The Dominance of Florence

At the beginning of the 15th century, when the Visconti rulers of Milan were threatening to overrun Florence, the humanist chancellor Coluccio Salutati had rallied the Florentines by reminding them that their city was "the daughter of Rome" and the heir of Roman justice and liberty. Salutati's pupil, Leonardo Bruni, who also served as chancellor, took up this line in his praise of Florence and in his *Historiarum Florentini populi libri XII* ("Twelve Books of Histories of the Florentine People"). Even before the rise of Rome, according to Bruni, the

The 500th anniversary of the publication of *The Prince* was celebrated at the National Central Library of Florence in 2013.

Assessing Machiavelli

The term "Machiavellian" refers to someone who is unscrupulous, cunning, cynical, and unprincipled. The adjective would have dismayed Niccolò Machiavelli, from whose name it is derived. He was one of the brightest lights of the Italian Renaissance, a writer of powerful, influential, and thoughtful prose who was devoted to truth and to the freedom of Florence, the city he loved. However, his chief works, *The Prince* and *Discourses on the First Ten Books of Titus Livy*, have been interpreted as advocating for political maneuvers marked by cunning, duplicity, or bad faith.

Still, some philosophers of the 17th and 18th centuries defended Machiavelli. The English lawyer and philosopher Francis Bacon (1561–1626) discussed Machiavelli in his *The Essayes or Counsels, Civill and Morall* (1625), noting his boldness. The English political philosopher James Harrington (1611–77), in his *The Common-wealth of Oceana* (1656), speaks admiringly of Machiavelli as the "prince of politicians" and the disciple of ancient prudence. The Dutch-Jewish philosopher Benedict de Spinoza (1632–77) defended Machiavelli's good intentions in teaching tyrants how to gain power, claiming in his *Political Treatise* (1677) that Machiavelli was a republican. Likewise, the French philosopher Jean-Jacques Rousseau (1712–78) asserted in his *Social Contract* (1762) that Machiavelli was, despite appearances, "an honest man and a good citizen" and *The Prince* "the book of republicans."

But the greater, more fundamental claim of Machiavelli's influence is as the founder of modernity. Machiavelli himself despised the moderns of his day as weak, but he also held forth the possibility of a "perpetual republic" that would remedy the weakness of the moderns. He imagined that such a republic would correct the errors of the Romans and so establish a political order no longer subject to the changes of fortune. There is no modern science in Machiavelli, but he does allude to many other modern notions, such as irreversible progress, secularism, and obtaining public good through private interest.

Etruscans had founded free cities in Tuscany, so the roots of Florentine liberty went very deep. There, equality was recognized in justice and opportunity for all citizens, and the claims of individual excellence were rewarded in public offices and public honours. This close relation between freedom and achievement, argued Bruni, explained Florence's superiority in culture as well as in politics. Florence was the home of Italy's greatest poets, the pioneer in both vernacular and Latin literature, and the seat of the Greek revival and of eloquence. In short, Florence was the centre of the *studia humanitatis*.

As political rhetoric, Bruni's version of Florentine superiority was magnificent and no doubt effective. It inspired the Florentines to hold out against Milanese aggression and to reshape their identity as the seat of "the rebirth of letters" and the champions of freedom. But, as a theory of political culture, this "civic humanism," as Hans Baron has called it, represented the ideal rather than the reality of 15th-century communal history. Even in Florence, where after 1434 the Medici family held a grip on the city's republican government, opportunities for the active life began to fade. The emphasis in thought began to shift from civic humanism to Neoplatonist idealism and to the kind of utopian mysticism represented by Pico's *Oration on the Dignity of Man*. At the end

Florence in the mid- to late-15th century, as shown here, was ruled by Medici princes in all but name.

of the century, Florentines briefly put themselves into the hands of the millennialist Dominican preacher Fra Girolamo Savonarola, who envisioned the city as the "New Jerusalem" rather than as a reincarnation of ancient Rome. Still, even Savonarola borrowed from the civic tradition of the humanists for his political reforms (and for his idea of Florentine superiority) and in so doing created a bridge between the republican past and the crisis years of the early 16th century.

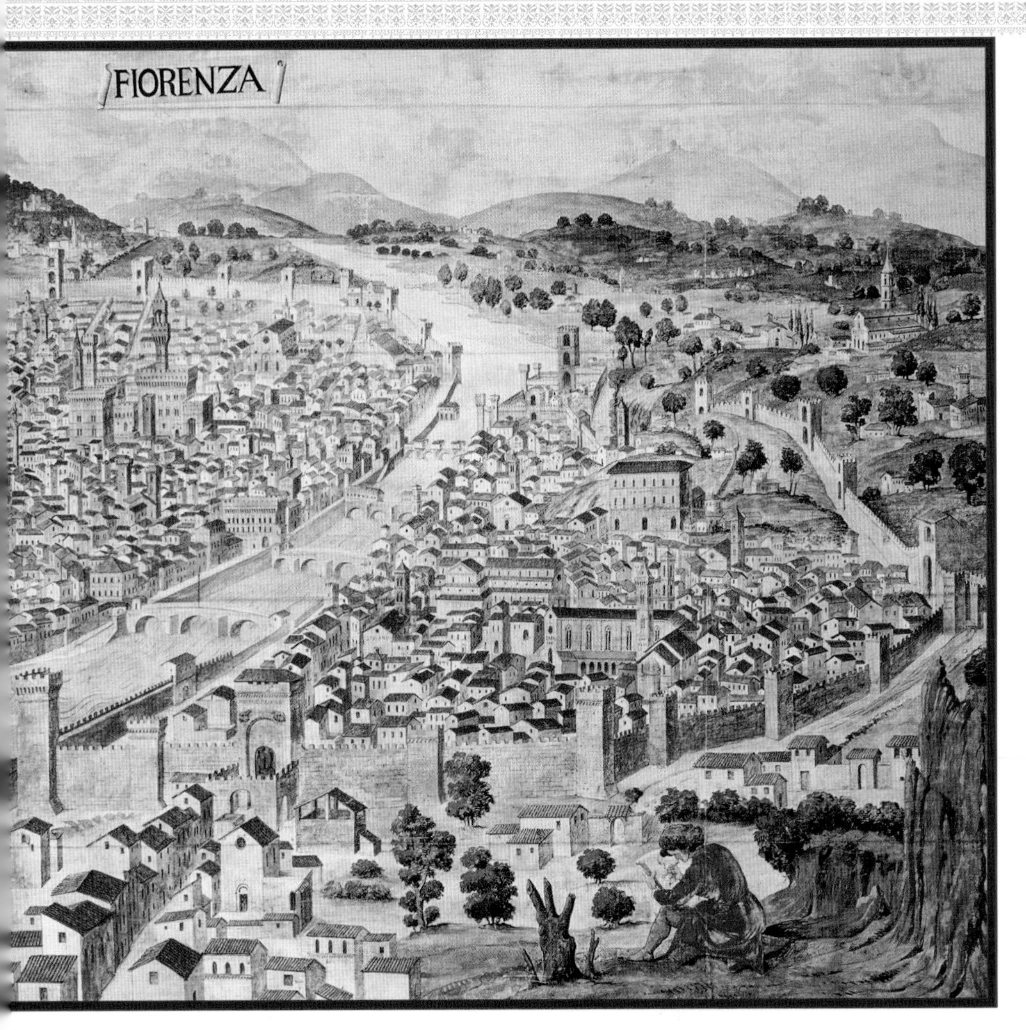

Machiavelli got his first job in the Florentine chancellery in 1498, the year of Savonarola's fall from power. Dismissing the friar as one of history's "unarmed prophets" who are bound to fail, Machiavelli was convinced that the principles of Christianity had helped make the Italian states sluggish and weak. He regarded religion as an indispensable component of human life, but statecraft as a discipline based on its own rules and no more to be subordinated to Christianity

Leonardo Bruni's Latin translations of many classical Greek works, including those of Plato, Aristotle, and Plutarch, furthered the study of Greek literature in the West.

than were jurisprudence or medicine. The simplest example of the difference between Christian and political morality is provided by warfare, where the use of deception, so detestable in every other kind of action, is necessary, praiseworthy, even glorious. In the *Discourses*, Machiavelli commented upon a Roman defeat:

> *This is worth noting by every citizen who is called upon to give counsel to his country, for when the very safety of the country is at stake there should be no question of justice or injustice, of mercy or cruelty, of honour or disgrace, but putting every other consideration aside, that course should be followed which will save her life and liberty.*

Machiavelli's own country was Florence; when he wrote that he loved his country more than he loved his soul, he was consciously forsaking Christian ethics for the morality of civic virtue.

Guicciardini and *The History of Italy*

Machiavelli's friend and countryman Francesco Guicciardini shared his political morality and his concern for politics but lacked his faith that a knowledge of ancient political wisdom would redeem the liberty of Italy. Guicciardini was an upper-class Florentine who chose a career in public administration and devoted his leisure to writing history and reflecting on politics. He was steeped in the humanist traditions of Florence and was a dedicated republican, notwithstanding the fact—or perhaps because of it—that he spent his entire career in the service of the Medici and rose to high positions under them. But Guicciardini, more skeptical and aristocratic than Machiavelli, was also half a generation younger, and he was schooled in an age that was already witnessing the decline of Italian autonomy.

In 1527, Florence revolted against the Medici a second time and established a republic. As a confidant of the Medici, Guicciardini was passed over for public office and retired to his estate. One of the fruits of this enforced leisure was the so-called *Cose fiorentine (Florentine Affairs)*, an unfinished manuscript on Florentine history. While it generally follows the classic form of humanist civic history, the fragment contains some significant departures from this tradition. No longer is the history of the city treated in isolation: Guicciardini was becoming aware that the political fortunes of Florence were interwoven with those of Italy as a whole and that the French invasion of Italy in 1494 was a turning point in Italian history. He returned to public life with the restoration of the Medici in 1530 and was involved in the events leading to the tightening of the imperial grip upon Italy, the humbling of the papacy, and the final transformation of the republic of Florence into a hereditary Medici dukedom.

Frustrated in his efforts to influence the rulers of Florence, he again retired to his villa to write. But, instead of taking up the unfinished manuscript on Florentine history, he chose a subject matching his changed perspective on Italian affairs. The result was his *History of Italy*. Though still in the humanist form and style, it was in substance a fulfillment of the new tendencies already evident in the earlier work—criticism of sources, great attention to detail, avoidance of moral generalizations, shrewd analysis of character and motive.

1

Libro Primo

Io ho deliberato di scriuere le cose accadute alla memoria nra
in Jtalia, dapoi che l'arme de Franzesi chiamate da nri Prinçi
pi medesimi cominciorono con grandissimo mouimento a pertur
barla: materia per la uarieta & grandezza loro, molto memora
bile; et piena di atrocissimi accidenti, hauendo patito tanti anni
Jtalia, tutte quelle Calamita, con le quali sogliono i miseri morta
li, hora per l'ira giusta di Jddio, hora dalla impieta & scelera
tezze degl'altri huomini, essere uessati. Dalla Cognitione de
quali casi, tanto uarij, & tanto graui, potra ciascuno, et per se
proprio, & per bene publico, prendere molti salutiferi documenti,
onde per innumerabili exempli euidentemente apparira a questa quanta
instabilita, ne altrimenti che uno mare concitato da venti, siano
sottoposte le cose humane, quanto siano pernitiosi el piu delle quasi sempre
uolte a se stessi, ma sempre a popoli i consigli male misurati di
coloro, che dominano, quando hauendo solamente innanzi agli
occhi, o errori uani, o le cupidita presenti, non si ricorda
do delle spesse uariationi della fortuna, & conuertendo in de
trimento altrui [illegible] conceduta loro, per la salute comune,
si fanno, o per poca prudentia, o per troppa ambitione auttori
di nuoue perturbationi. Ma le calamita di Italia, accioche io
faccia noto quale fussi allhora lo stato suo, et insieme le ca
gioni dalle quali hebbono origine tanti mali, cominciorono

Gucciardini's *History of Italy* is the most important contemporary history of Italy from the Renaissance.

The *History of Italy* has rightly been called a tragedy by the American historian Felix Gilbert, for it demonstrates how, out of stupidity and weakness, people make mistakes that gradually narrow the range of their freedom to choose alternative courses and thus to influence events until, finally, they are trapped in the web of fortune. This view of history was already far from the world of Machiavelli, not to mention that of the civic humanists. Where Machiavelli believed that *virtù*—bold and intelligent initiative—could shape, if not totally control, *fortuna*—the play of external forces—Guicciardini was skeptical about men's ability to learn from the past and pessimistic about the individual's power to shape the course of events. All that was left, he believed, was to understand. Guicciardini wrote his histories of Florence and of Italy to show what people were like and to explain how they had reached their present circumstances. Human dignity, then, consisted not in the exercise of will to shape destiny but in the use of reason to contemplate and perhaps to tolerate fate. In taking a new, hard look at the human condition, Guicciardini represents the decline of humanist optimism.

Chapter Four

The Northern Renaissance

In 1494 King Charles VIII of France led an army southward over the Alps, seeking the Neapolitan crown and glory. He found the Kingdom of Naples easy to take and impossible to hold. Frightened by local uprisings, by a new Italian coalition, and by the massing of Spanish troops in Sicily, he left Naples in the spring of 1495, never to return to Italy.

Conceived amid dreams of chivalric glory and crusade, the Italian expedition of Charles VIII was the venture of a medieval king—romantic, poorly planned, and totally irrelevant to the real needs of his subjects. The French invasion of Italy marked the beginning of a new phase of European politics, during which the Valois kings of France and the Habsburgs of Germany fought each other, with the Italian states as their reluctant pawns.

The Italian Wars

For the next 60 years the dream of Italian conquest was pursued by every French king, none of them having learned anything from Charles VIII's misadventure except that the road southward was open and paved with easy victories. For even longer Italy would be the keystone of the arch that the Habsburgs tried to erect across Europe from the Danube to the Strait of Gibraltar in order to link the Spanish and German inheritance of the emperor Charles V. In destroying the autonomy of Italian politics, the invasions also ended the Italian state system, which was absorbed into the larger European system that now took shape. Its members adopted the balance-of-power diplomacy first evolved by the Italians as well as the Italian practice of using resident ambassadors who combined diplomacy with the gathering of intelligence by fair means or foul. In the art of war, also, the Italians were innovators in the use of mercenary troops, cannonry, bastioned fortresses, and field fortification. French artillery was already the best in Europe by 1494, whereas the Spaniards developed the tercio, an infantry unit that combined the most effective field fortifications and weaponry of the Italians and Swiss.

Thus, old and new ways were fused in the bloody crucible of the Italian Wars. Rulers who lived by medieval codes of chivalry adopted Renaissance techniques of diplomacy and warfare to satisfy their lust for glory and dynastic power. Even the lure of Italy was an old obsession; but the size and vigour of the 16th-century expeditions were new. Rulers were now able to command vast quantities of men and resources because they were becoming masters of their own domains. The nature and degree of this mastery varied according to local circumstances. But throughout Europe

The French marched through the republic of Genoa in northern Italy on their way to capturing the kingdom of Naples in February 1495.

the New Monarchs, as they are called, were reasserting kingship as the dominant form of political leadership after a long period of floundering and uncertainty.

By the end of the 15th century, the Valois kings of France had expelled the English from all their soil except the port of Calais, concluding the Hundred Years' War (1453). They had incorporated the fertile lands of the duchy of Burgundy to the east and of Brittany to the north, and they had extended the French kingdom from the Atlantic and the English Channel to the Pyrenees and the Rhine. To rule this vast territory, they created a professional machinery of

The Battle of Pavia on February 24, 1525, was the decisive military engagement of the war in Italy between Francis I of France and the Habsburg emperor Charles V. The French army of 28,000 was virtually annihilated.

state: converting wartime taxing privileges into permanent prerogative, freeing their royal council from supervision by the Estates-General, appointing a host of officials who criss-crossed the kingdom in the service of the crown and establishing their right to appoint and tax the French clergy. They did not achieve anything like complete centralization. Still, as Jean Bodin wrote in 1576, in his *Six Books of the Commonwealth*, the king of France had absolute sovereignty because

he alone in the kingdom had the power to give law unto all of his subjects in general and to every one of them in particular.

Centralized Monarchies and Economic Growth

The founding of the mighty Spanish empire went back more than a century to 1469, when Ferdinand II of Aragon and Isabella of Castile brought two great Hispanic kingdoms together under a single dynasty. Castile, an arid land of sheepherders, great landowning churchmen, and crusading knights, and Aragon, with its Catalan miners and its strong ties to Mediterranean Europe, made uneasy partners. However, a series of rapid and energetic actions forced the process of national consolidation and catapulted the new nation into a position of world prominence for which it was poorly prepared. Within the last decade of the 15th century, the Spaniards took the kingdom of Navarre in the north; stormed the last Muslim stronghold in Spain, the kingdom of Granada; and launched a campaign of religious unification by pressing tens of thousands of Muslims and Jews to choose between baptism and expulsion, at the same time establishing a new Inquisition under royal control. They also sent Columbus on voyages of discovery to the Western Hemisphere, thereby opening a new frontier just as the domestic frontier of reconquest was closing. Finally, the crown linked its destinies with the Habsburgs by a double

This wood relief depicts the forced baptism of Moors (Spanish Muslims) in the kingdom of Granada, in modern-day southern Spain.

marriage, thus projecting Spain into the heart of European politics.

In the following decades, Castilian hidalgos (lower

nobles), whose fathers had crusaded against the Moors in Spain, streamed across the Atlantic to make their fortunes out of the land and sweat of the American Indians, while others marched in the armies and sailed in the ships of their king, Charles I. As Charles V, he was elected Holy Roman emperor in 1519 at the age of 19. In this youth, the vast dual inheritance of the Spanish and Habsburg empires came together. The grandson of Ferdinand and Isabella on his mother's side and of the emperor Maximilian I on his father's, Charles was duke of Burgundy, head of five Austrian dukedoms (which he ceded to his brother), king of Naples, Sicily, and Sardinia, and claimant to the duchy of Milan as well as king of Aragon and Castile and German king and emperor. To administer this enormous legacy, he presided over an ever-increasing bureaucracy of viceroys, governors, judges, military captains, and an army of clerks. The New World lands were governed by a separate Council of the Indies after 1524, which, like Charles' other royal councils, combined judicial, legislative, military, and fiscal functions.

The yield in American treasure was enormous, especially after the opening of the silver mines of Mexico and what is now Bolivia halfway through the 16th century. The crown skimmed off a lion's share—usually a fifth—which it paid out immediately to its creditors because everything Charles could raise by taxing or borrowing was sucked up by his wars against the French in Italy and Burgundy, the Protestant princes in Germany, the Turks on the Austrian border, and the Barbary pirates in the Mediterranean. By 1555, both Charles and his credit were exhausted, and he began to relinquish his titles—Spain and the Netherlands to his son Philip, Germany and the imperial title to his brother

This portrait of Charles V dates from 1519, the year he became Holy Roman emperor.

Ferdinand I. American silver did little for Spain except to pay the wages of soldiers and sailors; the goods and services that kept the Spanish armies in the field and the ships afloat were largely supplied by foreigners, who reaped the profits. Yet, for the rest of the century, Spain continued to dazzle the world, and few could see the chinks in the armour: this was an age of kings, in which bold deeds, not balance sheets, made history.

The growth of centralized monarchy claiming absolute sovereignty over its subjects may be observed in other places, from the England of Henry VIII to the Muscovite tsardom of Ivan III the Great in modern-day Russia. The New Monarchy was one aspect of a more general phenomenon—a great recovery that surged through Europe in the 15th century. No single cause can be determined to explain it. Some historians believe it was simply the upturn in the natural cycle of growth: the great medieval population boom had overextended Europe's productive capacities; the depression of the 14th and early 15th centuries had corrected this condition through famines and epidemics, leading to depopulation; and thus now the cycle of growth was beginning again.

Once more, growing numbers of people, burgeoning cities, and ambitious governments were demanding food, goods, and services—a demand that was met by both old and new methods of production. Several factors contributed to the decline of an agricultural system based on manors: the shift toward commercial crops such as wool and grains, the investment of capital, and the emancipation of servile labour. (In eastern Europe, however, the formerly free peasantry was now forced into serfdom by an alliance between the mon-

This 15th-century painting depicts silk makers in Lyon, which by the 17th century would become the silk-manufacturing capital of Europe.

archy and the landed gentry, as huge agrarian estates were formed to raise grain for an expanding Western market.) Manufacturing boomed, especially of those goods used in the outfitting of armies and fleets: cloth, armour, weapons, and ships. New mining and metalworking technology made it possible to exploit the rich iron, copper, gold, and silver deposits of central Germany, Hungary, and Austria, affording the opportunity for large-scale investment of capital.

One index of Europe's recovery is the spectacular growth of certain cities. Antwerp, for example, more than doubled its population in the second half of the 15th century and doubled it again by 1560. Under Habsburg patronage, Antwerp became the chief European entry port for English cloth, the hub of an international banking network, and the principal Western market for German copper and silver, Portuguese spices, and Italian alum. By 1500 the Antwerp Bourse was the central money market for much of Europe. Other cities profited from their special circumstances, too: Lisbon as the home port for the Portuguese maritime empire; Sevilla (Seville), the Spaniards' gateway to the New World; London, the capital of the Tudors and gathering point for England's cloth-making and banking activity; Lyon, favoured by the French kings as a market centre and capital of the silk industry; and Augsburg, the principal north-south trade route in Germany and the home city of the Fugger merchant-bankers.

Northern Humanism

Cities were also markets for culture. The resumption of urban growth in the second half of the 15th century coincided with the diffusion of Renaissance ideas and educational values. Humanism offered linguistic and rhetorical skills that were becoming indispensable for nobles and commoners seeking careers in diplomacy and government administration. Moreover, the Renaissance ideal of the perfect gentleman was a cultural style that had great appeal in this age of growing courtly refinement. At first many who wanted a humanist education went to Italy, and many foreign names appear on the rosters of the Italian universities. By the end of the century, however, such northern cities as London, Paris, Antwerp, and Augsburg were becoming centres of humanist activity rivaling Italy's. The development of printing, by making books cheaper and more plentiful, also quickened the diffusion of humanism.

Although Italian humanism is often considered to be mostly secular, Italian Lorenzo Valla was the first to show how the critical methods used to study the classics ought to be applied to problems of biblical interpretation and translation as well as church history. This program began to be carried out in the 16th century, particularly in the countries of northern Europe (and Spain). Before that, few scholars had the necessary skills, particularly the knowledge of Greek. By the early 1500s, Greek was a regular part of the humanist curriculum, and Hebrew was becoming much better known, particularly after Johannes Reuchlin published his Hebrew grammar in 1506. Here, too, printing was a crucial factor, for it made available a host of lexicographical and grammatical handbooks and allowed the establishment of normative biblical texts and the comparison of different versions of the Bible.

Christian humanism was more than a program of scholarship, however. It was fundamentally a conception of the Christian life that was grounded in the rhetorical, historical, and ethical orientation of humanism itself. It was inspired by factors such as the spiritual stresses of rapid social change and the inability of the ecclesiastical establishment to cope with the religious needs of an increasingly literate and self-confident laity. By restoring the gospel to the centre of Christian piety, the humanists believed they were better serving the needs of ordinary people. They attacked scholastic theology as a dry intellectualization of simple faith, and they deplored the tendency of religion to become a ritual practiced vicariously through a priest. They also despised

Desiderius Erasmus was the greatest scholar of the northern Renaissance, the first editor of the New Testament, and also an important figure in classical literature.

the whole late-medieval apparatus of relic mongering, hagiology, indulgences, and image worship, and they ridiculed it in their writings, sometimes with devastating effect.

According to the Christian humanists, the fundamental law of Christianity was the law of love as revealed by Jesus Christ in the Gospel. Love, peace, and simplicity should be the aims of the good Christian, and the life of Christ his perfect model. The chief spokesman for this point of view was Desiderius Erasmus, the most influential humanist of his day. Erasmus and his colleagues were uninterested in dogmatic differences and were early champions of religious toleration. In this they were not in tune with the changing times, for the outbreak of the Reformation polarized European society. As a result, the Christian humanists, who had done so much to lay the groundwork for religious reform, ended by being suspect on both sides. The Roman Catholics considered them subversives who laid the groundwork for reformers such as Martin Luther. The Protestants, meanwhile, thought the Christian humanists were hypocrites who had abandoned the cause of reformation out of cowardice or ambition.

CHRISTIAN MYSTICS

The religious impulse that gave rise to Christian humanism was also manifested in a variety of forms of religious devotion among the laity, including mysticism. In the 14th century, a wave of mystical ardour seemed to course down the valley of the Rhine, enveloping men and women in the rapture of intense, direct experience of the divine Spirit. It centred in the houses of the Dominican order, where friars and nuns practiced the mystical way of their great teacher, Meister Eckhart. This wave of Rhenish mysticism radiated beyond convent walls to the marketplaces and hearths of the laity. Eckhart had the gift of making his obscure doctrines understandable to a wider public than was usual for mystics.

In the Netherlands, the mystical impulse awakened chiefly under the stimulus of another great teacher, Gerhard Groote. Not a monk nor even a priest, Groote gave the mystical movement a different direction by teaching that true spiritual communion must be combined with moral action, for this was the whole lesson of the Gospel. At his death, a group of followers formed the Brethren of the Common Life. These were laymen and laywomen, married and single, earning their livings in the world but united by a simple rule that required them to pool their earnings and devote themselves to spiritual works, teaching, and charity. Houses of Brothers and Sisters of the Common Life spread through the cities and towns of the Netherlands and Germany. The Brethren were particularly successful as schoolmasters, combining some of the new linguistic methods of the humanists with a strong emphasis upon Bible study. Among the generations of children who absorbed the new piety (*devotio moderna*) in their schools were Erasmus and, briefly, Luther.

One man whose life was changed by *The Imitation* was the 16th-century Spaniard Ignatius of Loyola. After reading it, Loyola

continued on the next page

continued from the previous page

founded the Society of Jesus and wrote his own book of methodical prayer, *Spiritual Exercises*. Thus, Spanish piety was in some ways connected with that of the Netherlands. However, the extraordinary outburst of mystical and contemplative activity in 16th-century Spain was mainly an expression of the intense religious exaltation of the Spanish people themselves as they confronted the tasks of reform, Counter-Reformation, and world leadership. Spanish mysticism belies the usual picture of the mystic as a withdrawn contemplative, with his or her head in the clouds. In addition to Loyola, St. Teresa of Avila and her disciple, St. John of the Cross, were tough, activist Reformers who regarded their mystical experiences as a means of fortifying themselves for their practical tasks. They were also prolific writers who could communicate their experiences and analyze them for the benefit of others.

The Growth of Vernacular Literature

In literature, medieval forms continued to dominate the artistic imagination throughout the 15th century. Besides the vast devotional literature of the period—the *ars moriendi*, or books on the art of dying well, the saints' lives, and manuals of methodical prayer and spiritual consolation—the most popular reading of noble and burgher alike was a 13th-century love allegory, the *Roman de la rose*. Despite a promising start in the late Middle Ages, literary creativity suffered from the domination of Latin as the language of "serious" expression. If the vernacular attracted writers, they tended to overload it

Geoffrey Chaucer's *Canterbury Tales*, written in Middle English in the late 14th century, ranks as one of the greatest poetic works in English.

with Latinisms and artificially applied rhetorical forms. This was the case with the so-called *grands rhetoriqueurs* of Burgundy and France. One exception is 14th-century England, where a national literature made a brilliant showing in the works of William Langland, John Gower, and, above all, Geoffrey Chaucer. The troubled 15th century, however, produced only feeble imitations. Another exception is the vigorous tradition of chronicle writing in French, distinguished by such eminently readable works as the chronicle of Jean Froissart and the memoirs of Philippe de Commynes. In France, too, about the middle of the 15th century there lived the vagabond François Villon, a great poet about whom next to nothing is known. In Germany *The Ship of Fools*, by Sebastian Brant, was a lone masterpiece.

The 16th century saw a true renaissance of national literatures. In Protestant countries, the Reformation had an enormous impact upon the quantity and quality of literary output. Luther's rebellion had destroyed the chances of unifying the nation politically, because religious division exacerbated political division and made Lutherans intolerant of the Catholic Habsburgs. However, his translation of the Bible into German created a national language. Biblical translations, vernacular liturgies, hymns, and sacred drama had analogous effects elsewhere. For Roman Catholics, especially in Spain, the Reformation was a time of deep religious emotion expressed in art and literature. On all sides of the religious controversy, chroniclers and historians writing in the vernacular were recording their versions for posterity.

While the Reformation was providing a subject matter, the Italian Renaissance was providing literary methods and models. The Petrarchan sonnet inspired French, English,

Miguel de Cervantes is the most important and celebrated figure in Spanish literature.

and Spanish poets, while the Renaissance neoclassical drama finally began to end the reign of the medieval mystery play. Ultimately, of course, the works of real genius were the result of a crossing of native traditions and new forms. The Frenchman François Rabelais assimilated all the themes of his day—and mocked them all—in his story of the giants Gargantua and Pantagruel. The Spaniard Miguel de Cervantes, in *Don Quixote,* drew a composite portrait of his countrymen, which caught their exact mixture of idealism and realism. In England, Christopher Marlowe and William Shakespeare used Renaissance drama to probe the deeper levels of their countrymen's character and experiences.

CHAPTER FIVE

RENAISSANCE SCIENCE AND TECHNOLOGY

Out of the ferment of the Renaissance and Reformation there arose a new view of science that brought about many transformations, including the reeducation of common sense in favour of abstract reasoning; the substitution of a quantitative for a qualitative view of nature; and the view of nature as a machine rather than as an organism. Scientists of this era also developed an experimental method that sought definite answers to certain limited questions couched in the framework of specific theories. They accepted new criteria for explanation, stressing the "how" rather than the "why" that had characterized the Aristotelian search for final causes. All of these changes brought great advances in many fields. Science became an autonomous discipline, distinct from both philosophy and technology.

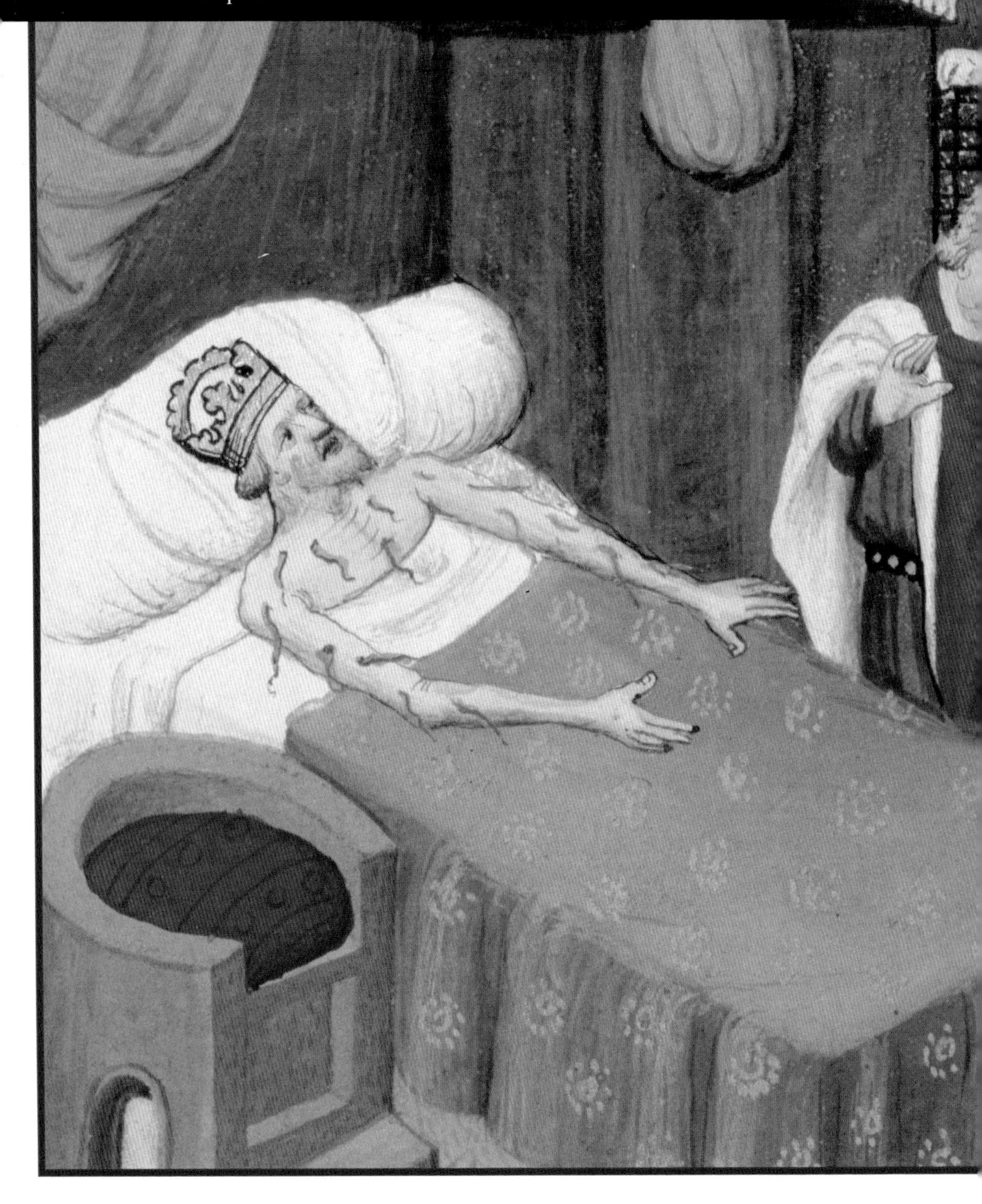

Leeching, the application of a living leech to the skin in order to initiate blood flow or deplete blood from a localized area of the body, was a common medical practice in medieval times.

Science in Medieval Times

According to medieval scientists, matter was composed of four elements—earth, air, fire, and water—whose combinations and permutations made up the world of visible objects. The cosmos was a series of concentric spheres in motion, the farther ones carrying the stars around in their daily courses. At the centre was the globe of Earth, heavy and static. Motion was either perfectly circular, as in the heavens, or irregular and naturally downward, as on Earth. The Earth had three landmasses—Europe, Asia, and Africa—and was unknown and uninhabitable in its southern zones. Human beings, the object of all creation, were composed of four humours—black and yellow bile, blood, and phlegm—and the body's health was determined by the relative proportions of each. The cosmos was alive with a universal consciousness with which people could interact in various ways. The heavenly bodies were generally believed to influence human character and events, although theologians worried about free will.

These views were an amalgam of Classical and Christian thought and, from what can be inferred from written sources, shaped the way educated people experienced and interpreted phenomena. What people who did not read or write books understood about nature is more difficult to tell, except that belief in magic, good and evil spirits, witchcraft, and forecasting the future was universal. The church might prefer that Christians seek their well-being through faith, the sacraments, and the intercession of Mary and the saints, but distinctions between acceptable and unacceptable belief in hidden powers were difficult to make or to maintain. Most clergy shared the common beliefs in occult forces and lent their authority to them. The collaboration of formal doctrine and popular belief had some of its most terrible consequences during the Renaissance, such as pogroms against Jews and witch-hunts. The church provided the doctrines of Satanic conspiracy, and the inquisitorial agents and popular prejudice supplied the victims, predominantly women and marginal people.

The ideas of Aristotle had dominated scientific thought for almost 2,000 years, and they were only very slowly dismantled, beginning during the Renaissance era. Among the formally educated, if not among the general population, traditional science was transformed by the new heliocentric, mechanistic, and mathematical conceptions. Historians of science are increasingly reluctant to describe these changes as a "revolution," since this implies too sudden and complete an overthrow of the earlier model. Still, the Renaissance made some important contributions to science. Humanist scholarship provided both originals and translations of ancient Greek scientific works—which enormously increased the fund of knowledge in physics, astronomy, medicine, botany, and other disciplines—and presented alternative theories to those of Ptolemy and Aristotle. Renaissance philosophers, most notably Jacopo Zabarella, analyzed and formulated the rules of the deductive and inductive methods by which scientists worked, while certain ancient philosophies enriched the ways in which scientists conceived of phenomena.

The Heliocentric System

The revival of ancient science also brought heliocentric astronomy to the fore again after almost two millennia. In the 5th century BCE the Greek philosophers Philolaus and Hicetas speculated separately that the Earth was a sphere revolving daily around some mystical "central fire" that regulated the universe. Two centuries later, Aristarchus of Samos extended this idea by proposing that the Earth and other planets moved around a definite central object, which he believed to be the Sun.

The heliocentric, or Sun-centred, model of the solar system never gained wide support because its proponents could not explain why the relative positions of the stars seemed to remain the same despite the Earth's changing viewpoints as it moved around the Sun. In the 2nd century AD, Claudius Ptolemy of Alexandria suggested that this discrepancy could be resolved if it were assumed that the Earth was fixed in position, with the Sun and other bodies revolving around it. As a result, Ptolemy's geocentric (Earth-centred) system dominated scientific thought for some 1,400 years. In 1444 Nicholas of Cusa again argued for the rotation of the Earth and of other heavenly bodies, but it was not until *De revolutionibus orbium coelestium libri VI* ("Six Books Concerning the Revolutions of the Heavenly Orbs") in 1543 that the heliocentric system began to be reestablished.

Copernicus probably began to suspect that Earth should be regarded as one of the planets that revolved around the Sun sometime between 1508 and 1514. For years, however, he delayed publication of his controversial work, which contradicted all the authorities of the time. *De revolutionibus orbium*

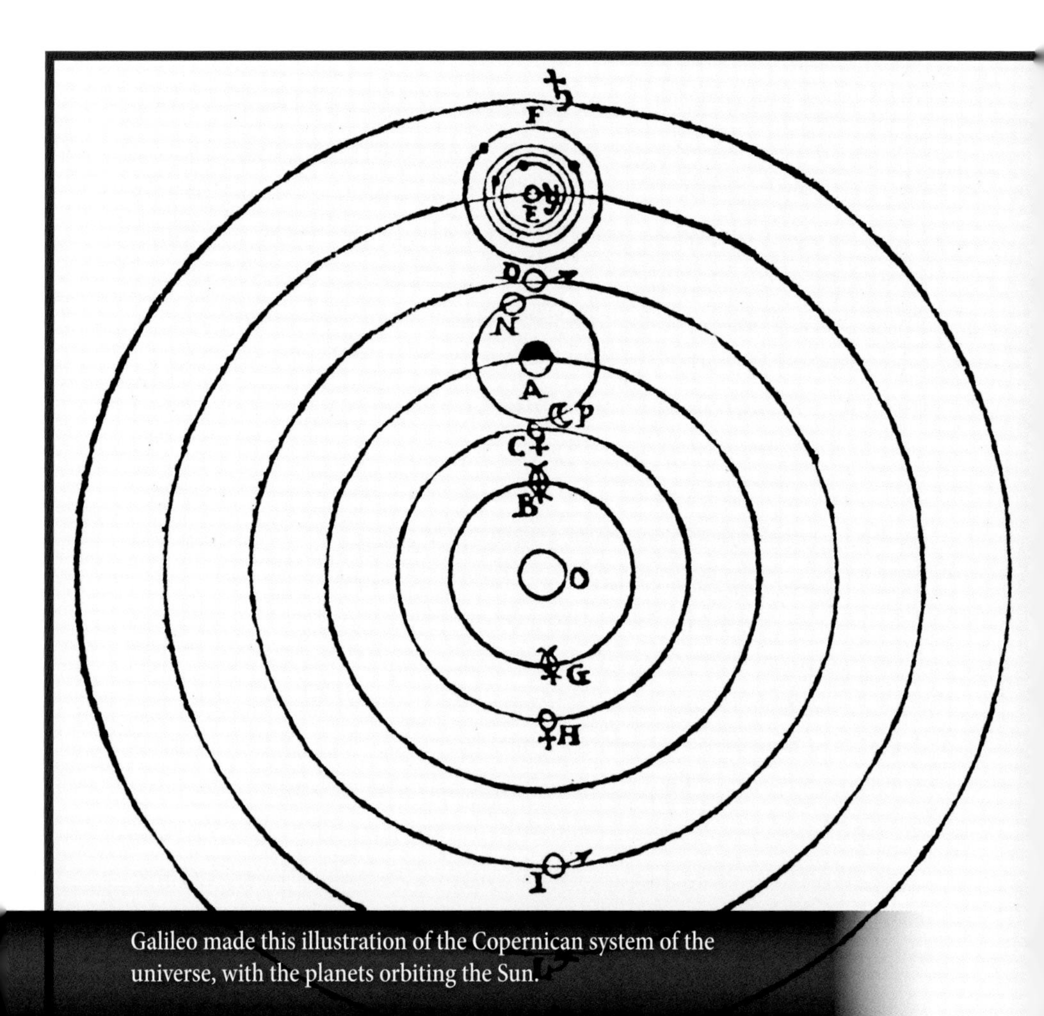

Galileo made this illustration of the Copernican system of the universe, with the planets orbiting the Sun.

coelestium libri vi did not appear in print until 1543, the year of his death. According to legend, Copernicus received a copy a few days after he lost consciousness from a stroke, awakening to realize that he was holding his great book before he expired on May 24. The book opened the way to a truly scientific approach to astronomy. It had a profound influence on later thinkers of the scientific revolution, including such major figures as Galileo, Johannes Kepler, and Isaac Newton.

MATHEMATICS

In mathematics the Renaissance made its greatest contribution to the rise of modern science. Italian artists and merchants influenced mathematics in several ways. In the 15th century a group of Tuscan artists, including Filippo Brunelleschi, Leon Battista Alberti, and Leonardo da Vinci, incorporated linear perspective into their practice and teaching, about a century before mathematicians formally treated the subject. Italian *maestri d'abbaco* tried, albeit unsuccessfully, to solve nontrivial cubic equations. In fact, the first general solution was found by Scipione del Ferro at the beginning of the 16th century and rediscovered by Niccolò Tartaglia several years later. The solution was published by Gerolamo Cardano in his *Ars magna (Ars Magna or the Rules of Algebra)* in 1545, together with Lodovico Ferrari's solution of the quartic equation.

By 1380 an algebraic symbolism had been developed in Italy in which letters were used for the unknown, for its square, and for constants. The symbols used today for the unknown (for example, x), the square root sign, and the signs + and – came into general use in southern Germany beginning about 1450. They were used by Regiomontanus

Renaissance Man

The term "Renaissance man" was coined to describe the genius of Leonardo da Vinci. He was a man of so many accomplishments in so many areas of human endeavor that his like has rarely been seen in human history. "Renaissance man" is now used to refer to a person who is accomplished in many fields.

Casual patrons of the arts know da Vinci as the painter of *La Gioconda*, more commonly called the *Mona Lisa*, and of the exquisite *Last Supper*, painted on the wall of the dining hall in the monastery of Santa Maria delle Grazie in Milan, Italy. These paintings alone would have assured him enduring fame as an artist, but he was also a sculptor, an architect, and a man of science who did serious investigations into the natural and physical sciences, mathematics, mechanics, and engineering. An artist by disposition and endowment, he considered his eyes to be his main avenue to knowledge. To da Vinci, sight was man's highest sense because it alone

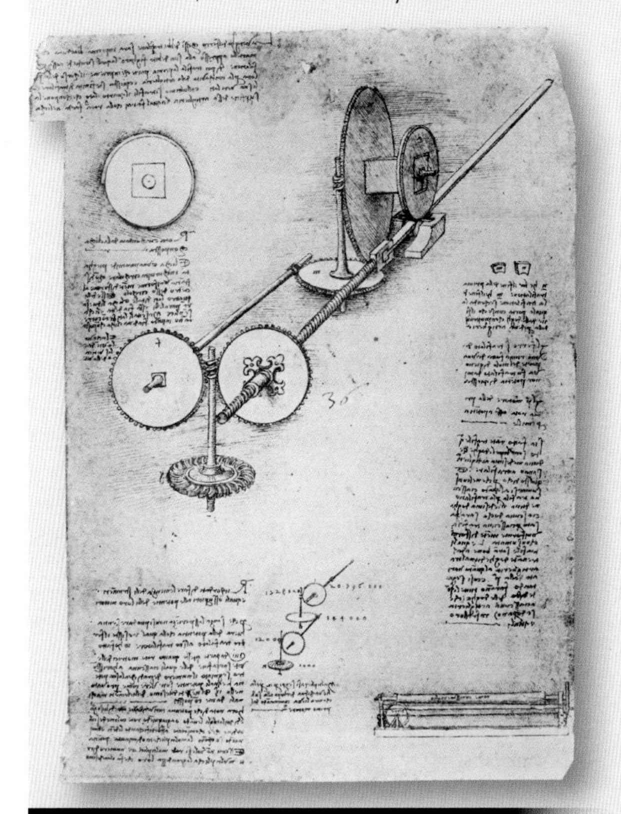

A page from one of Leonardo da Vinci's notebooks shows the operation of a mechanical wing.

conveyed the facts of experience immediately, correctly, and with certainty. Hence, every phenomenon perceived became an object of knowledge, and *saper vedere* ("knowing how to see") became the great theme of his studies.

More than 300 years before flying machines were perfected, da Vinci devised plans for prototypes of an airplane and a helicopter. His extensive studies of human anatomy were portrayed in anatomical drawings, which were among the most significant achievements of Renaissance science. His remarkable illustrations of the human body elevated drawing into a means of scientific investigation and exposition and provided the basic principles for modern scientific illustration.

and by Fridericus Gerhart and received an impetus about 1486 at the University of Leipzig from Johann Widman. The idea of distinguishing between known and unknown quantities in algebra was first consistently applied by François Viète, with vowels for unknown and consonants for known quantities. Viète found some relations between the coefficients of an equation and its roots. This was suggestive of the idea, explicitly stated by Albert Girard in 1629 and proved by Carl Friedrich Gauss in 1799, that an equation of degree n has n roots. Complex numbers, which are implicit in such ideas, were gradually accepted about the time of Rafael Bombelli (died 1572), who used them in connection with the cubic.

If they had done nothing else, Renaissance scholars would have made a great contribution to mathematics by translating and publishing, in 1544, some previously

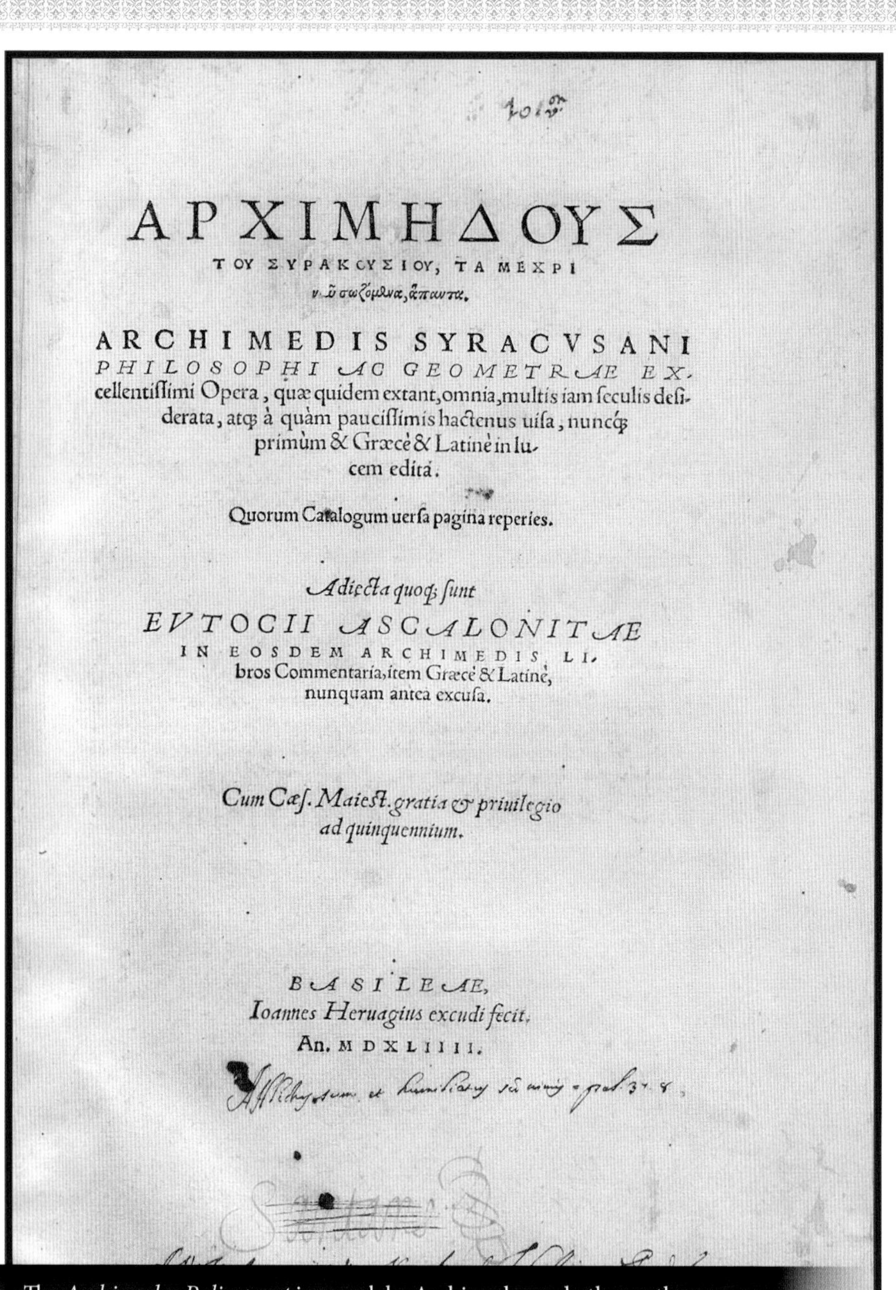
ΑΡΧΙΜΗΔΟΥΣ

ΤΟΥ ΣΥΡΑΚΟΥΣΙΟΥ, ΤΑ ΜΕΧΡΙ
νῦν σωζόμενα, ἅπαντα.

ARCHIMEDIS SYRACVSANI
PHILOSOPHI AC GEOMETRAE EX-
cellentissimi Opera, quæ quidem extant, omnia, multis iam seculis desi-
derata, atque à quàm paucissimis hactenus uisa, nuncque
primùm & Græcè & Latinè in lu-
cem edita.

Quorum Catalogum uersa pagina reperies.

Adiecta quoque sunt
EVTOCII ASCALONITAE
IN EOSDEM ARCHIMEDIS LI-
bros Commentaria, item Græcè & Latinè,
nunquam antea excusa.

Cum Cæs. Maiest. gratia & priuilegio
ad quinquennium.

BASILEAE,
Ioannes Heruagius excudi fecit.
An. MDXLIIII.

The *Archimedes Palimpsest* is a work by Archimedes and other authors that was copied in the Byzantine Empire in the 10th century. This printed edition dates from the 16th century.

unknown works of Archimedes, perhaps the most important of the ancients in this field. Apollonius's *Conics* and the investigations of areas (quadratures) and of volumes (cubatures) by Archimedes formed part of the humanistic learning of the 16th century. These studies strongly influenced the later developments of analytic geometry, the infinitesimal calculus, and the theory of functions, subjects that were developed in the 17th century.

WARFARE

Warfare was one catalyst of practical change that stimulated new theoretical questions. With the spread of the use of artillery, for example, questions about the motion of bodies in space became more insistent, and mathematical calculation more critical.

The earliest known gunpowder weapons vaguely resembled an old-fashioned soda bottle or a deep-throated mortar and pestle. The earliest such weapon, depicted in the English de Millimete manuscript, was some three feet long with a bore diameter of about two inches (five centimetres). The projectile resembled an arrow with a wrapping around the shaft, probably of leather, to provide a gas seal within the bore. Firing was apparently accomplished by applying a red-hot wire to a touchhole drilled through the top of the thickest part of the breech. The gun was laid horizontally on a trestle table without provision for adjusting elevation or absorbing recoil—a tribute to its modest power, which would have been only marginally greater than that of a large crossbow.

The breakthrough that led to the emergence of true cannon derived from three basic perceptions. The first was that gunpowder's propellant force could be used most effectively by confining it within a tubular barrel. This stemmed from an awareness that gunpowder's explosive energy did not act instantaneously upon the projectile but had to develop its force across time and space. The second perception was that methods of construction derived from cooperage could be used to construct tubular wrought-iron gun barrels. The

Large artillery pieces such as this cannon first appeared in Europe in the 15th century, but until about 1670 the word "cannon" was applied only to special types of guns.

third perception was that a spherical ball was the optimal projectile. The result was modern artillery.

Small arms did not exist as a distinct class of gunpowder weapon until the middle of the 15th century. Until then, hand cannon differed from their larger relatives only in size. They looked much the same, consisting of a barrel fastened to a simple wooden stock that was braced beneath the gunner's arm. A second person was required to fire the weapon. About the middle of the 15th century, a series of connected developments established small arms as an important and distinct category of weaponry. The first of these was the development of slow match—or match, as it was commonly called. This was cord or twine soaked in a solution of potassium nitrate and dried. When lit, match smoldered at the end in a slow, controlled manner. Slow match found immediate acceptance among artillerists and remained a standard part of the gunner's kit for the next four centuries.

The manufacture of guns also stimulated metallurgy and fortification. The Renaissance preoccupation with alchemy, the parent of chemistry, was certainly stimulated by the shortage of precious metals, made more acute by the expansion of government and expenditures on war.

The Printing Press

The most important technological advance of all, because it underlay progress in so many other fields, strictly speaking, had little to do with nature. This was the development of printing with movable metal type around the mid-15th century in Germany. Johannes Gutenberg is usually called its inventor, but in fact many people and many steps were

LU

Lucas sirus natione anthiocensis arte medicus discipulus apostolorum postea paulum secutus usque ad confessionem eius serviens domino sine crimine: nam neque uxorem umquam habuit neque filios: septuaginta et quatuor annorum obiit in bithinia plenus spiritu sancto. Qui cum iam scripta essent evangelia per matheum quidem in iudea per marcum autem in italia: sancto instigante spiritu in achaie partibus hoc scripsit evangelium: significans etiam ipse in principio ante suum alia esse descripta. Cui extra ea que ordo evangelice dispositionis exposcit ea maxime necessitas laboris fuit: ut primum grecis fidelibus omni prophetatione venturi in carnem dei cristi manifestata humanitate ne iudaicis fabulis attenti: in solo legis desiderio tenerentur: vel ne hereticis fabulis et stultis solicitationibus seducti exciderent a veritate elaboraret: dehinc ut in principio evangelii iohannis nativitate presumpta cui evangelium scriberet et in quo electus scriberet indicaret: contestans in se completa esse que essent ab aliis incohata. Cui ideo post baptismum filii dei a perfectione generationis in cristo implete repetende a principio nativitatis humane potestas permissa est: ut requirentibus demonstraret in quo apprehendens erat per nathan filium david introitu recurrentis in deum generationis admisso indisparabilis dei predicans in hominibus cristum suum perfecti opus hominis redire in se per filium faceret: qui per david patrem venientibus iter prebebat in cristo. Cui luce non inmerito etiam scribendorum actuum apostolorum potestas in ministerio datur: ut deo in deum pleno et filio perditionis extincto oratione ab apostolis facta sorte domini electionis numerus compleretur: sicque paulus consummationem apostolicis actibus daret quem diu contra stimulum recalcitrantem dominus elegisset. Quod et legentibus ac requirentibus deum et si per singula expediri a nobis utile fuerat: sciens tamen quod operantem agricolam oporteat de suis fructibus edere vitavimus publicam curiositatem: ne non tam volentibus deum demonstrare videremur quam fastidientibus prodidisse.

Incipit evangelium secundum lucam. Prohemium ipsius beati luce in evangelium suum.

Quoniam quidem multi conati sunt ordinare narrationes que in nobis complete sunt rerum sicut tradiderunt nobis qui ab initio ipsi viderunt et ministri fuerunt sermonis: visum est et michi assecuto omnia a principio diligenter ex ordine tibi scribere optime theophile: ut cognoscas eorum verborum de quibus eruditus es veritatem.

Fuit in diebus herodis regis iudee sacerdos quidam nomine zacharias de vice abia et uxor illi de filiabus aaron: et nomen eius elizabeth. Erant autem iusti ambo ante deum: incedentes in omnibus mandatis et iustificationibus domini sine querela. Et non erat illis filius eo quod esset elizabeth sterilis: et ambo processissent in diebus suis. Factum est autem cum sacerdotio fungeretur zacharias in ordine vicis sue ante deum: secundum consuetudinem sacerdotii sorte exiit ut incensum poneret ingressus in templum domini. Et omnis multitudo populi erat orans foris hora incensi. Apparuit autem illi angelus domini: stans a dextris altaris

This copy of Gutenberg's Forty-two-line Bible, first printed in Mainz, Germany, about 1455, dates from the 15th century.

involved. Block printing on wood came to the West from China between 1250 and 1350. Papermaking came from China by way of the Arabs in 12th-century Spain. The Flemish technique of oil painting was the origin of the new printers' ink. Three men of Mainz—Gutenberg and his contemporaries Johann Fust and Peter Schöffer—seem to have taken the final steps, casting metal type and locking it into a wooden press. The invention spread like the wind, reaching Italy by 1467, Hungary and Poland in the 1470s, and Scandinavia by 1483. By 1500 the presses of Europe had produced some 6 million books.

Without the printing press it is impossible to conceive that the Reformation would have ever been more than a monkish quarrel or that the rise of a new science, which was a cooperative effort of an international community, would have occurred at all. In short, the development of printing amounted to a communications revolution of the order of the invention of writing. Like that prehistoric discovery, it transformed the conditions of life. The communications revolution immeasurably enhanced human opportunities for enlightenment and pleasure on one hand and created previously undreamed-of possibilities for manipulation and control on the other.

Conclusion

The Renaissance witnessed the discovery and exploration of new continents, the substitution of the Copernican for the Ptolemaic system of astronomy, the decline of the feudal system and the growth of commerce, and the invention or application of such potentially powerful innovations as paper, printing, the mariner's compass, and gunpowder. To the scholars and thinkers of the day, however, it was primarily a time of the revival of Classical learning and wisdom after a long period of cultural decline and stagnation. In the course of striving to recover ancient wisdom, the humanists assisted in the consolidation of a new spiritual and intellectual outlook and in the development of a new body of knowledge. The effect of humanism was to help men break free from the mental strictures imposed by religious orthodoxy, to inspire free inquiry and criticism, and to inspire a new confidence in the possibilities of human thought and creations.

From Italy the new humanist spirit and the Renaissance it engendered spread north to all parts of Europe, aided by the invention of printing, which allowed literacy and the availability of Classical texts to grow explosively. The intellectual stimulation provided by humanists helped spark the Reformation (though many humanists, including Erasmus, did not approve of the Reformation). By the end of the 16th century the battle of Reformation and Counter-Reformation had commanded much of Europe's energy and attention, while the intellectual life was poised on the brink of the Enlightenment.

Glossary

ARTILLERY Crew-served carriage-mounted firearms, such as cannons, used in modern warfare that are of calibre greater than that of small arms.

BALANCE-OF-POWER DIPLOMACY An equilibrium or adjustment of power between potentially opposing sovereign states such that neither state is willing or able to upset that equilibrium by waging war or interfering with the interests of the other.

EPISTLE A composition in prose or poetry written in the form of a letter.

FEUDAL Of, relating to, or having the characteristics of a medieval fief: founded upon or involving the relation of lord and vassal with tenure of land.

HAGIOLOGY Literature dealing with venerated persons or writings.

HUMANISM The learning or cultural impulse that flowered during the Renaissance and is characterized by a revival of classical letters, an individualistic and critical spirit, and a shift of emphasis from religious to secular concerns.

HUMOUR A normal functioning fluid or semifluid of the body (as the blood, lymph, or bile).

LAY Belonging or relating to those not in holy orders; not of the clergy.

LITURGY A rite or series of rites, observances, or procedures prescribed for public worship in the Christian church.

MERCANTILISM Economic theory and practice common in Europe from the 16th to the 18th century that promoted governmental regulation of a nation's economy for the purpose of augmenting state power at the expense of rival national powers.

MYSTICISM The doctrine or belief that direct knowledge of God is attainable through subjective experience (as immediate intuition, insight, or illumination).

POGROM An organized massacre of helpless people usually with the connivance of officials; usually applied to attacks on Jews in the Russian Empire in the late 19th and early 20th centuries.

PREEMINENT Having paramount rank, dignity, or importance.

PREROGATIVE A right attached to an office or rank to exercise a special privilege or function.

REPUBLICANISM Adherence to or sympathy for a republican form of government, in which the state is ruled by representatives of the citizen body.

RHETORIC The art of expressive speech or discourse.

SECULAR Of or relating to the worldly or temporal as distinguished from the spiritual or eternal; not sacred.

SOVEREIGNTY Supreme power especially over a political body.

TREATISE A writing (as a book or article) that treats a subject in a systematic manner.

VERNACULAR Using a language or dialect native to a region or country rather than a literary, cultured, or foreign language.

UNSCRUPULOUS Unprincipled; having no moral integrity.

Bibliography

The Italian Renaissance

Lauro Martines, *Power and Imagination: City-States in Renaissance Italy* (1979, reissued 1988), provides an informative survey. Florentine history is authoritatively surveyed in Gene Brucker, *Renaissance Florence* (1969, reissued 1983). Eric Cochrane, *Florence in the Forgotten Centuries, 1527–1800: A History of Florence and the Florentines in the Age of the Grand Dukes* (1973), ventures beyond the fall of the Florentine republic. Venetian history is ably treated in D.S. Chambers, *The Imperial Age of Venice, 1380–1580* (1970); William H. McNeill, *Venice: The Hinge of Europe, 1081-1797* (1974, reprinted 1986); and Robert Finlay, *Politics in Renaissance Venice* (1980).

Social and cultural conditions and religious life are approached in Brian Pullan, *Rich and Poor in Renaissance Venice: The Social Institutions of a Catholic State, to 1620* (1971); Richard C. Trexler, *Public Life in Renaissance Florence* (1980); David Herlihy and Christiane Klapisch-Zuber, *Tuscans and Their Families: A Study of the Florentine Catasto of 1427* (1985; originally published in French, 1978); Ronald F.E. Weissman, *Ritual Brotherhood in Renaissance Florence* (1982); Edward Muir, *Civic Ritual in Renaissance Venice* (1981); and Donald E. Queller, *The Venetian Patriciate: Reality Versus Myth* (1986). Joan Kelly, "Did Women Have a Renaissance?" in her *Women, History & Theory* (1984), challenged Burckhardt's thesis that women achieved equality with men in Renaissance Italy. Other good studies on women in the Renaissance include Ian Maclean, *The Renaissance Notion of Woman: A Study in the Fortunes of Scholasticism and Medical Science in European Intellectual Life* (1980); Christiane Klapisch-Zuber, *Women, Family, and Ritual in Renaissance Italy*, trans. from French (1985); and Margaret W. Ferguson, Maureen Quilligan, and

Nancy J. Vickers (eds.), *Rewriting the Renaissance: The Discourses of Sexual Difference in Early Modern Europe* (1986). Samuel Kline Cohn, Jr., *The Laboring Classes in Renaissance Florence* (1980), is a controversial groundbreaking study.

A good starting point for the study of Renaissance intellectual history is Paul Oskar Kristeller, *Renaissance Thought: The Classic, Scholastic, and Humanistic Strains*, rev. ed. (1961), and *Renaissance Thought II: Papers on Humanism and the Arts* (1965, reissued 1980). Eugenio Garin, *Italian Humanism: Philosophy and Civic Life in the Renaissance*, trans. from Italian (1965, reprinted 1975); and Hans Baron, *The Crisis of the Early Italian Renaissance: Civic Humanism and Republican Liberty in an Age of Classicism and Tyranny*, rev. ed. (1966), treat humanism as a civic ethos as well as a scholarly and educational movement; while Charles Trinkaus, *In Our Image and Likeness: Humanity and Divinity in Italian Humanist Thought*, 2 vol. (1970), disproves the notion of humanism as primarily secular. Ernest H. Wilkins, *Life of Petrarch* (1961), provides information on the acknowledged founder of Renaissance humanism. Ronald G. Witt, *Hercules at the Crossroads: The Life, Works, and Thought of Coluccio Salutati* (1983), is an excellent study of a figure second only to Petrarch in importance. George Holmes, *Florence, Rome, and the Origins of the Renaissance* (1986), revives an old thesis attributing the origins of the Renaissance to the age of Dante.

Studies of humanist culture outside Florence include J.K. Hyde, *Padua in the Age of Dante* (1966); John F. D'Amico, *Renaissance Humanism in Papal Rome: Humanists and Churchmen on the Eve of the Reformation* (1983); Charles L. Stinger, *The Renaissance in Rome* (1985); Jerry H. Bentley, *Politics and Culture in Renaissance Naples* (1987); and Margaret L. King, *Venetian Humanism in an Age of Patrician Dominance* (1986). A lively revisionist view that challenges basic assumptions about the history of Renaissance humanism is presented in Anthony Grafton and Lisa Jardine, *From Humanism to the Humanities: Education and the Liberal Arts in Fifteenth- and Sixteenth-Century Europe* (1986). Albert Rabil, Jr. (ed.), *Renaissance Humanism: Foundations, Forms, and Legacy*, 3 vol. (1988); Lauro Martines, *Power and Imagination: City States in Renaissance Italy* (1988); and Donald Kelley, *Renaissance Humanism* (1991), discuss the current state of studies on humanism.

The classic account of the development of diplomacy is Garrett Mattingly, *Renaissance Diplomacy* (1955, reprinted 1988); the subject is also discussed in Joycelyne G. Russell, *Peacemaking in the Renaissance* (1986). Michael Mallett, *Mercenaries and Their Masters: Warfare in Renaissance Italy* (1974), is a study of war in the Renaissance. Felix Gilbert, *Machiavelli and Guicciardini: Politics and History in Sixteenth-Century Florence* (1965, reprinted 1984), provides the political and cultural context of the thought of two leading Renaissance political scholars. J.G.A. Pocock, *The Machiavellian Moment: Florentine Political Thought and the Atlantic Republican Tradition* (1975), traces the Renaissance heritage to modern times. Sebastian de Grazia, *Machiavelli in Hell* (1989), is a fresh, lively intellectual biography of the great Florentine.

SCIENCE AND TECHNOLOGY

Elizabeth L. Eisenstein, *The Printing Press as an Agent of Change: Communications and Cultural Transformations in Early Modern Europe*, 2 vol. (1979), and *The Printing Revolution in Early Modern Europe* (1983), make a strong case for the revolutionary impact of Renaissance print technology upon culture. The concept of a "scientific revolution" is upheld in such standard works as Herbert Butterfield, *The Origins of Modern Science: 1300–1800*, rev. ed. (1957, reprinted 1982); I. Bernard Cohen, *From Leonardo to Lavoisier, 1450–1800* (1980); and A. Rupert Hall, *The Revolution in Science, 1500–1750*, 3rd ed. (1983); while the continuities with medieval science are stressed in A.C. Crombie, *Medieval and Early Modern Science*, 2nd rev. ed. (1959, reissued 1967). Feminist theorists have made some influential contributions to revisionist perspectives deploring the "triumphalism" with which scientific advance has been treated: for example, Evelyn Fox Keller, *Reflections on Gender and Science* (1985); Margaret Jacobs and James Jacobs, *The Cultural Meaning of the Scientific Revolution* (1988); and Londa Schiebinger, *The Mind Has No Sex: Women in the Origins of Modern Science* (1989).

THE RENAISSANCE OUTSIDE ITALY

New areas of investigation in social history, including the history of the lower classes, women, the family, and popular religion, are exemplified in Emmanuel Le Roy Ladurie, *The Peasants of Languedoc* (1974; originally published in French, 1966); Peter Laslett, *The World We Have Lost: Further Explored*, 3rd. ed. (1984); Natalie Zemon Davis, *Society and Culture in Early Modern France* (1975, reissued 1987); Peter Burke, *Popular Culture in Early Modern Europe* (1978, reprinted 1988); Richard Kieckhefer, *European Witch Trials: Their Foundations in Popular and Learned Culture, 1300–1500* (1976); Steven Ozment, *When Fathers Ruled: Family Life in Reformation Europe* (1983); Joseph Klaits, *Servants of Satan: The Age of the Witch Hunts* (1985); and Brian P. Levack, *The Witch-Hunt in Early Modern Europe* (1987).

In religious history there has been a tendency to reconstruct the bridges between the late medieval and Reformation piety and thought. Among the most influential examples of this effort are Heiko Augustinus Oberman, *The Harvest of Medieval Theology: Gabriel Biel and Late Medieval Nominalism* (1963, reissued 1983); and Heiko Augustinus Oberman (ed.), *Forerunners of the Reformation: The Shape of Late Medieval Thought* (1966, reissued 1981). Other important studies include Steven E. Ozment (ed.), *The Reformation in Medieval Perspective* (1971); and Thomas N. Tentler, *Sin and Confession on the Eve of the Reformation* (1977).

Another, not necessarily contradictory, tendency has been that of seeing the history of late medieval and Renaissance religion on its own terms, rather than as the prelude to the Reformation; this approach is taken by Charles Trinkaus and Heiko Augustinus Oberman (eds.), *The Pursuit of Holiness in Late Medieval and Renaissance Religion* (1974); and Richard Kieckhefer, *Unquiet Souls: Fourteenth-Century Saints and Their Religious Milieu* (1984). An original and valuable, if sometimes debatable, overview is John Bossy, *Christianity in the West, 1400–1700* (1985).

HISTORIOGRAPHICAL PROBLEMS

Jacob Burckhardt, *The Civilization of the Renaissance in Italy* (1890; originally published in German, 1860), is a classic work, elegant and stimulating, available in many later editions, but its thesis, that 14th-century Italians broke sharply with their medieval past to create modern states and a highly individualistic secular society and culture, has been heavily modified by most modern specialists. Wallace K. Ferguson, *The Renais-*

sance in Historical Thought: Five Centuries of Interpretation (1948, reprinted 1981), offers an excellent introduction, but recent scholarship has expanded the range and depth of knowledge and dissolved such interpretive consensus as still existed when Ferguson wrote. E.F. Jacob (ed.), *Italian Renaissance Studies* (1960); Tinsley Helton (ed.), *The Renaissance: A Reconsideration of the Theories and Interpretations of the Age* (1961, reprinted 1980); and Denys Hay, *The Italian Renaissance in Its Historical Background*, 2nd ed. (1977), characterize the interpretations of the 1960s. At present most Renaissance historians do not make the sweeping characterizations of the "spirit of an age" that once came so easily. An excellent historiographical and bibliographical guide to works about Europe outside Italy is Steven Ozment (ed.), *Reformation Europe: A Guide to Research* (1982), not really limited to the Reformation.

Index